Black Mothers
HOLD THE LINE
Collection, Vol. 2

Edited by Dominique J. Smiley

ISBN: 978-0-9836364-2-7(Paperback)

Front cover image & design by Saheran Shoukat

Printed in the United States of America.

First printing edition 2022.

Out of the Ashes, LLC
2931 Ogletown Rd.
Neward. DE 19713
http://www.outoftheashesllc.com/

Lord, what is it you want us to hear?
We sit here quietly waiting, but the message isn't clear!

Let our hurt know it's not against us, it's for us.
You didn't send it to break us, but to make us.

Let the loneliness we feel, know You are here and
If we only open up our heart, we would feel You near.

Let our depression know joy will come
If we trust and believe in the One in whom it's from.

Lord, all of this is easier said than done,
It takes our mental to a place where we want to run.

So, we **Pause** to take a deep breath, we **Process** in an attempt to put our mind at rest, we **Pray** in hopes that you will hear our cry and then we **Proceed** in Faith, thanking You with every step, for Your mercy & grace.

Lord, is this what You wanted us to hear?
As we sit here quietly, the message is becoming clear.

We thank You for your endless love for us,
As we become the women you called us to be, it's in Your guiding presence that we Trust!

Written By
Patty Harris
4.5.2017 (original written)
11.27.2021 (revised)

CHAPTERS

"I am a human, I have feelings, I am not confirming, I am vulnerable"

Shane' Darby, "Pain to Power" ♦ *V1*

UNDERSTANDING THE JOURNEY FROM THE INSIDE OUT

Patricia D. Harris

Prior to COVID, my husband and I traveled often and as much as I enjoyed it, I was never a big fan of flying. So, in days prior to us leaving, I would pray heavily for our safe travel, the pilot, the flight attendants, and the other passengers on the plane. I would pray for a smooth takeoff and a smooth landing. And if I'm honest, while that brought me great peace, one thing that also brought me comfort was having my husband by my side. We'd board the plan and as soon as I heard, "Flight Attendants prepare for takeoff," I'd immediately grab his hand and would hold it for dear life until we were safely in the air. While I continued to pray during periods of turbulence, my husband's presence continued to bring me a great sense of peace. But on October 17, 2021, as I sat at the Philadelphia Airport, Terminal 12, waiting for a 2 p.m. flight, I was alone. This weighed heavily on me–the thought of taking this trip on my own–and as much as I needed this trip, it frightened me. Yes, I prayed as I have always done, but the difference on this trip was my husband would not be with me. As much as I wanted him there, that somehow God would work it out for him to come or should I say give him a desire to come with me, I knew in my heart of hearts, I had to take this trip alone. I needed a mental break and as much as I was also hoping to get an emotional break, I found my emotions still very much all over the place.

This summer, we had a lot of exciting things take place; our daughter turned 21 and our middle son got married two days apart from one another, and yes, we celebrated both of them as if they were years apart. Then, a month or so later, my brother got married, and all three beautiful events took place in my backyard! Thank God for the support of one of my closest girlfriends because, without her, I would not have been able to pull all of it off. So, this summer was a very happy time and while the smiles and laughter should have all been very easy, if I'm honest, it was not. It was very draining. See, when you are going through one of the toughest storms in your life, still trying to show up as your best self, trying to remain faithful while keeping the faith, it is very taxing on your mind, body, and spirit. This is where I found myself and the reason for this trip. I needed a break, but most importantly, I needed time away and to be restored by God. I needed a spiritual awakening. I didn't know what that would look like or how it was going to come. I just knew I wanted to get away and rest in God's arms with no interruptions. This was a trip where all my trust had to be in God. It would be His hand that I would hold on to and it would be His arms I would rest in.

Queens, I feel like I am in the fight of my life, and although I have committed to holding the line, there are moments of fear, loneliness, and deep disappointed that overtake me. While I'm not giving up, I find myself in need of a separation from what has become my norm. Sometimes you must step away from the fight to be reminded of who you are, who you belong to, and why this fight is so important. You have to go back and ask, "*God, what is it You want me to do? God, please remind me of the weapons You have given me to get through! God, this thing seems so much bigger than what I can handle. I need help!*" And watch Him meet you right where you are.

I can relate to when Jesus said, "Father, if you are willing, let this cup pass from me. However, not my will, but yours be done." I know you may be wondering how I could have the audacity to even compare myself to what Jesus went through because He paid the ultimate price. And to a certain extent, you would be right in asking. He paid a bill that none of us could ever pay. But if I am being honest with myself and you, this is something I have asked more than once. It has been 18 months since the separation from my husband shook my world. During one of the most unfamiliar times we have ever seen in our lives with the onset of COVID, I had to watch the man that I love walk out the door.

On March 9, 2020, the world shutdown and June 26, 2020, my world blew up–well, at least that's what it felt like. To hear the words, "I'm leaving" shook me to my core. And although God was preparing me for this very thing back in October 2017 and provided me with a 4-edged sword–*Pause, Process, Pray, and Proceed*–I still could not comprehend the words that came out his mouth and my heart broke in a million pieces. This was not easy for him either. I could see that it also affected him deeply to have those words part from his lips. I also believe it took everything he had to walk out the door. He took great pride in providing for our family and there was a sense of protection I felt from him that I hadn't felt since before my father passing. But on this day, there was a pulling away that I believe began long before he took action. I now know he contemplated leaving well before June 26, 2020, but it was on this day he mustered up the courage to do so. I had seen the internal battle within him. It was difficult to watch and even harder to fight. I made a mental list of all the reasons this made sense; his past, my past, and the quickness of our union–we were destined to fail, right? Man, I wish I would have stayed on my knees in prayer longer, turned down my plate a few more times and sought God for direction. Instead, I found myself fleeing, riding up and down the highway, sleeping in parking lots, and playing right into the enemy's hands. I would tell myself I don't have to put up with this, but what I should have been asking was, "*God, how do you want me to handle this?*"

We are still deep in this season of separation, with divorce very much on the table and while I am so grateful to still be standing, not to have lost my mind, I'm sure you can imagine that some days are still very difficult than others. It's during those days that I have asked *why me, what did I do to deserve this? How can I be in this place yet again?*

See, I was married before to my children's father, and he too decided to leave. So, I try to figure out what was wrong with me that I could have two men walk out on me. It *had* to be me, right? I am the common denominator. Because of these thoughts and the desperate need to understand, I sought help, found a therapist, and began weekly sessions. I appreciated the time I had with her, but those sessions were short lived, and it had nothing to do with her. I knew this thing was much bigger than myself and the spiritual connection I needed wasn't going to be found in these sessions (don't get me wrong, I strongly believe in the power of a therapist).

I am also grateful for the prayer warriors that have been and still are in my corner. I am also tremendously thankful the Queens (OQs) from Vol.1 of *Hold the Line.* Their transparency and vulnerability encouraged me so much. Through all the love, support, honesty, truthfulness, and God's guidance, I have found the courage to look internally, and put a name to that very thing that has plagued me for all of my life. And while different ones said, "it's not you, it's them," I believe it was that very question of *Why me, and how did I get here*, that opened the door for God to show me exactly why.

A lesson that I had to learn quickly was not to lean on my own understanding. In Proverbs 3:5-6, it says ***"Trust in the Lord with all thine heart; and lean not unto thine own understanding. In all thy ways acknowledge Him and He shall direct thy paths."*** When you are so used to leaning on your own understanding, trying to figure and work things out on your own, it is difficult to do anything else. That is, until you realize it's not by your might, nor by your power, but by God's Spirit. What I also knew to be true was that God's spirit resided inside of me and was just waiting for me to tap into it.

While being on this roller coaster ride and failing miserably at what God called me to do, there was a yearning within me to draw closer to

Him. From a little girl, I have always known Him, but now I wanted to know Him in a more intimate way. I knew I had to be more intentional about setting time aside for just the two of us. So, I created a space that belonged to just us by converting my oldest son's bedroom into my prayer room. While I know God is with me always and wherever I am, I wanted Him to know just how committed I was to growing my relationship with Him. I wanted Him to know how important He was to me and how desperately I wanted to learn how to reside in His presence–not visit, but take up shop, and this is where the true journey began.

He began showing me things in me that I had been holding on to for years–can you say 44 years? I had to take a minute and acknowledge the fact that I had some things inside of me that held me captive for a very long time, and it was time that I spoke those things out if I truly wanted God to use me. I once heard someone say, "***You can't tame what you don't name.***" It was time for me to put names to those things that I continued to sweep under the rug. I heard God say, "Reveal it; Once you reveal it, then you can release it, and once you release it, you can begin on a path of restoration." He continued to say, "There are things that only you queens are called to do, but you have to be in position in order to do so." I wondered what He meant and because God is not a God of confusion, He showed me exactly what He meant.

Now queens, I know what I am about to say next could lead you to believe that I am taking all the responsibility for my husband leaving, but that's not the case at all. Remember, I said I wanted to have a more intimate relationship with God? Well, He heard me, met me right where I was, and broke this journey down for me. See, when you decide to have a more intimate walk with God, He shows you things about yourself that aren't pretty and sometimes very difficult to swallow. In all honesty, this is what I've come to enjoy the most. Maybe it's the part of me that likes to be in control and although, while being on this journey, I'm not in control, I love that God shows me the things that I can change about myself with His help. There are more times that I would like to admit that I still turn my focus on my husband and ask why he is doing this or that. It's during those moments that God so lovingly reminds me that my focus isn't to be on my husband, but that this journey is about me drawing closer to Him.

As I shared earlier, I have always known God, but through this season of my life, I am falling in love with Him in a way I have never experienced, and it's beautiful. I love how patient and understanding He is with me, and through all my mess, He still loves me. It's through knowing this that he gives me the strength to stand on His word and His promises. I know what He has for me is for me, and there is no good thing that He will withhold from me. I know that the enemy's weapons may form, but they will not prosper. If it's a fight that enemy wants, then it's a fight he will get! I'm not fighting *for* victory–I am fighting *from* victory because I serve the greatest General of all, and I am already victorious. I have to remind myself of this very thing daily. As much as I would like to admit that I have mastered walking through this chapter of my life in peace, that I don't feel like a ship tossing back and forth, that every other day I don't feel like giving up, I really do. Then I am reminded that not only was I called for this, I was chosen, and I was chosen because God trusted me. These reminders refuel me as well as give me the courage and confidence to fight yet another day.

Queens, all my life I had the desire to be chosen, not only after all other options have been explored, but I wanted to be chosen from the door. I so strongly needed this fulfillment, like I needed air to breathe. This need caused me to act out of character, put myself in situations and places I had no business being in, and pursue relationships I should have never given a second thought to. And while I was seeking acceptance from boys at a young age and to men as I got older, I wish someone would have reminded me that **I am that good thing waiting to be found and I don't have to go looking**. What I didn't know then that I know now, is that *I have always been chosen by God*. There was never a doubt in His mind that I was the one, the one not only called but chosen. The apple of His eye and the one made in His Image. Oh, my Lord, what a beautiful feeling and such a hard lesson to learn! I believe once you know this to be true, the battle is half won. *And how do you win the other half of the battle*, you ask? Well, I'm still seeking God for that blueprint, and I believe as I remain in position to hear His soft and loving voice, He will lead me step by step. He reminds me He never said it would be easy, but if I trust Him with my whole heart and not to look to the left or the right but look to the hills in which cometh my help, it will be doable. ***Pause, Process, Pray, and Proceed***–the application of these words becomes more and more clear to me, and I am grateful to God for gifting them to me.

Queens, I know when we get married there is an understanding that it will take two for the marriage to work. We are not in the marriage alone and the success of the marriage doesn't rely on one individual. Therefore, I know the reason for our separation doesn't totally fall on me. But for me to grow and learn, I had to take some serious time to figure out how I got here. I recognize there were times I left my post, and it was during those times that I allowed the enemy to infiltrate my marriage and my home. As a wife and mother, there are some things that only I was called to do, such as stay in prayer and remain present in God's presence so I could recognize the enemy from far off, keep my family covered in prayer, and call out those things that I knew the enemy was trying to use against us. See, I thought I would win this battle with my words and sometimes with my silence. I also thought if I would leave the house or didn't come home, it would show him how much he hurt me when he did this very thing. When he would reach out to touch me and I denied him, I thought he would understand the tears I shed the many nights he wasn't there to hold and comfort me. The point I was missing was this thing would not be won in the flesh, but in the spirit with me on my knees crying out to God for His guidance. I now realize that the foundation can't be poured during the storm; it has to be laid well before the storm comes.

From our very first date, when my husband stretched back his hand for me to grab on to, I felt a sense of peace and protection that I have never felt from anyone besides my dad. When I felt that, I should have been thanking God for that peace and protection, asking Him to keep it and that it always remains in line with His will for our union. Instead,

I held on to my husband's actions during that moment for dear life and when things went left, the peace and protection I once felt from him was gone, and I felt lost, not understanding where my true peace and protection comes from. Sometimes we put our faith and trust in the wrong thing or person, and when things don't go the way we think they should, we don't know what to do. See, this all comes from the desire to be validated, loved, desired, and chosen by man and not by God. In a relationship, these things should be given freely, but I am learning that I first have to receive all that God is trying to give me so I can properly identify what it should look like from someone else.

Previously, I listed all the reasons why my husband leaving made sense and two of those reasons were our past and the quickness of our union. I guess it's true when they say your heart knows no time, it just knows the one that makes it skip a beat! This is exactly what I felt very early on, that despite our history and the healing that we both needed to do outside of one another, I believed there was nothing him and I couldn't get through. I thought what we laid pretty early on–like first date early on–was a solid foundation. We sat on the floor of his apartment (I loved that apartment) and poured out our hearts to one another, and this was all before going to dinner. Based on that conversation alone and the decision to still move forward, there was no way you could have convinced me that we would be here, in this place of separation. I knew my heart was weak. I knew the time was short, and maybe the odds were against us. I was and still willing to give it all I got, because he, not He, was my finally. While the desire of my heart is for my husband and I to reconcile, I have to admit that little girl still wanting to be chosen, is screaming inside. There was still a great work to be done inside of me and I'm pretty confident, based off what the Holy Spirit has revealed to me while on this journey, had I relied more on Him, shared the burdens of my heart with Him, allowed Him to wipe my tears at night, I would have heard His soft quiet voice providing me with clear direction on how to handle all that I was taking myself through. I feel very strongly this is why He blessed me with *Pause, Process, Pray and Proceed.* He needed me to hear loud and clear what He was saying! I now realize I put more confidence in who Coley and I were together, than I did in our God that created us. I'm so grateful for this lesson. This lesson alone has provided me with the strength and confidence needed to Hold the Line!

Queens, I ask, what are you holding on to? What are you seeking from others? What are those things that have held you hostage and have prevented you from holding the line on behalf of your marriage, your children, your families and/or your communities? Whatever it is queen, **reveal** it, **release** it into God's mighty hands, and allow Him to help you on your journey towards **restoration**. Queen, during times of difficulties, I want to encourage you to **pause** and take a deep breath, **process,** and put your mind at rest, **pray** knowing God will hear your cry, and then **proceed** in faith, thanking God for his mercy and grace.

Queen, I may not know you by name, but I know you in my heart. If you stretch forth your hand, I will reach back and grab hold. This is not by my might, nor by my power, but only by the Spirit of the Lord! Together, we shall hold the line!

QUEEN, THERE IS PURPOSE IN YOUR JOURNEY!

Patricia D. Harris

About Patricia D. Harris

Patricia D. Harris offers over 30+ years of administrative and planning experience, serving in various roles including Sales Manager, Chief Administrative Officer, Executive Assistant and more recently, Human Resource Coordinator. In March 2014, Patty was recognized by NABFEME's as one of Delaware's Women Trailblazers, and in June 2015 she was recognized as a "mirror" recipient with The Hilton, one of the highest honors given by Meyer and Jabara Management. Patty is the founder of Patricia D. Harris ~ Hospitality Brokerage Firm, an event planning business, co-owner of Out of the Ashes: Where a Seed Finds Life and non-profit organization, Delaware Family Restoration Services, where restoring families dealing with trauma stemming from incarceration is their primary focus and is the organizer of the Facebook Group "Black Mothers," where the vision for the first collaborative book project, "Hold the Line" was birthed! Patty has a heart for black mothers' mental, physical, emotional, and spiritual wellbeing. It is her ongoing goal to remain in position to be used by God, and as He continues to breath on her, she continues to breath on her Queen Sistahs!

"Be contagious and spread love, joy and peace."

Shariece "Sunshine" Beecham, "You Matter" ♦ *V1*

LOST AND FOUND

Jasmine Brown

I could cry tears of joy right now.
I chuckle as I close the door to my childhood bedroom;
It is incredible, how things turned out.
I 'm so grateful to be here,
to put my thoughts on paper,
to have soup and crackers for dinner,
to feel safe and joyful
concurrently with feeling unsettled and frightened.
My mind is at a sprinter's pace, attempting to process all that's transpired.
My body is pulsating with adrenaline.
My heart knows something I don't.
I can 't tell if I 'm experiencing anxiety or euphoria.

How am I supposed to process this?
Do I need to speak with a therapist?
Was what happened really that serious?
Should I go back to my normal routine so soon?

Acceptance;
I have to accept what just happened and
what I'm currently feeling
for what it is,
then let it pass.

If I can do that,
Which I know I can
Then I'll get through this with time and grace.

I'm able to see even more clearly that the decision I made was for the best.
I'm sitting with my feelings-
confronting them
understanding them
letting them pass.
I am not turning back;
remaining present inside of this fresh wound has healed it.
It has helped me conquer fears I didn't know I was holding on to.

Now is the time for the adventure to begin,
to embark on my journey and take the steps laid out for me.
Here's where I use my faith, courage, and self-esteem
to nurture and grow; to become my true self.
Remembering every step of the way that I am guided,
I am on the right path and creating a life that feels good to me.

I'm getting back in touch with myself
by infusing my life with all that nourishes my soul,
trusting myself,
fulfilling the commitments I've made to myself
and by loving myself
in all the ways I looked outside of myself for.

Jasmine Brown

About Jasmine Brown

Jasmine Brown is a young professional and former small business owner with a passion for creative arts. A graduate of University of Delaware in 2016, Jasmine has since worked in the for-profit and nonprofit sectors, serving in roles that aid in the health & wellbeing of the community. Presently, Jasmine works at a small black-owned business providing professional development services to organizations and academic institutions across the country. As a young woman navigating her late twenties, she is keeping her eyes and heart open for more than what she thought was possible.

"I refuse to have the reflections of people, places, and things determine this chapter of my life."

Dawn L. Pipkin, "The Journey Back to Me" ♦ *V1*

JIREH NISSI SINGER

Angell Hodges-Morris

"You're so foolish.... you really thought that marrying this man was going to make all your dreams come true. That a new life for you was going to come simply because you said, 'I do.' I'm laughing at you right now." My aunt's words cut like a knife while she snickered as she spoke. Everything in me wanted to slap the piss out of her right there in that kitchen. She always made it a point to sneak in an insult when the other women in the family were around, like she had room to talk about anything referring to a nuptial. What did she know about marriage? She was married and divorced six times and had no room to give anyone marital advice. Truth be told, none of my aunts or cousins in this room could really give solid advice on marital affairs, but the least of them, my aunt, was doing the most talking. But this one thing hit home: I was too dependent on this man I married.

Is it really love when a wife does things for her husband but the first chance he gets, he throws it in her face? Not making her feel like a wife, but a prostitute because he buys her gifts or does for her the way he told her he would? These were the questions I asked myself constantly. This couldn't be what a marriage is. One thing I knew, he wouldn't control me with his coins. I had my own and could make my own. What it would take is the discipline to say "no" to myself and the things I wanted. I didn't care if I had $20 in my account for the next two weeks; I didn't want a *thing* from him. It was such a turn off when anyone throws what they did for you in your face, knowing that most of the time they offered, and you didn't ask. But that was my fault for getting too comfortable. Even marriage comes at a price.

Now I was sitting here watching this old bitty stuff chips down her throat, trying to judge my life in front of all my other aunt's and female cousins. This was a tradition in this family of women, and although I could've been imagining it, it somehow ended with me as the topic of conversation. Here she was at another family reunion with the "coochie cronies" ready to put my marriage on the chopping block. It is funny how people forget things while they are judging you. This was the same woman who knew her trifling second husband was molesting me and her daughter when we were six and twelve years old. It was nothing we ever spoke of around here because she still did not believe it happened, and she certainly didn't believe it happened for four dreadful years to me and three for my cousin. It was as common in my life as "hello." Being touched by men and even women became as much a part of my life as getting my hair washed and braided every week. I swear if I didn't believe in hell, my first suicide attempt would have happened before I could even spell my name, Jireh. I suddenly snapped back into the present moment, almost falling off my stool at the kitchen island, my aunt still spewing her unpleasantries.

“This is why you're miserable now. You can't stop daydreaming! You been that way since you were little, constantly living in la-la land,” Aunt Bert, aka Aunt Yodel said. Us kids called her “Aunt Yodel” behind her back because that’s what she sounded like when she made love to her fourth husband when we were in middle school. It was the most disgusting sound ever known to man. I never understood why in God's creation any man wanted to hear a woman do that in bed, but even a hound dog needs a shot. I continued stirring the potato salad, trying to make sure the mayo was distributed evenly throughout.

"Jireh, you know what your problem is?" I rolled my eyes until they almost came out the socket.

“No, Aunt Yo- um...Bert, but I'm sure you are ready to take the opportunity to tell me,” I said.

“Your problem is you are spoiled. Been spoiled since you were young. Just because your Momma walked out, and we felt sorry for my brother for having to take you on his own, we spoiled you! Now you just think a man is supposed to be at your beck and call. You better treat that man right before someone comes along and swipes him from under your nose!” she said with a sarcastic cackle trying to air-high five anyone close to her. The ladies in the kitchen all had different looks on their faces; some in agreement, some in shame and embarrassment, some in awe and disbelief that she had no couth at all. I just looked at her in disgust, like she was a stinking pool of stomach acid after a long night of binge drinking. Everything in me wanted to knock that crooked Salt-N-Pepa, asymmetrical wig straight on her head, but I thought of my pastor's words, "It's not about what they say or do, but how you react."

I stared at her long and hard as the room went from muffled comments and snickers to funeral silence in a matter of seconds. Suddenly, all the words my pastor or any pastor had ever said totally evaded my thoughts or comprehension. Aunt Bert knew she went too far but felt her respect as an elder would make her untouchable.

"God, I need you because I am sick and tired of this woman. I have been dealing with her disrespect my entire life," I prayed to myself. As much as I didn't want to reciprocate what was always given to me, I had been provoked long enough. I raised up slowly off my barstool, feeling the breath of Hades on my neck, walked around the ten-foot, eight-seater island of Aunt Bea's kitchen with the potato salad bowl in hand. I went completely deaf. I could see movement around me; I could even see lips moving and facial expressions of horror, but also some of eager anticipation to see what was about to transpire, as I walked right towards Aunt Yodel.

Crash!

I smashed the glass bowl filled with some of the best potato salad I had ever made right in Aunt Yodel's face, and before she realized she was bleeding, I added a special ingredient of some gooey, slimy hawk spit. I watched her slide down the front of the stove, holding the right side of face as blood poured out of her cheekbone area and squirted out of the side of her head. This was the first time she was speechless for as long as I could remember. I was totally satisfied. As I stepped back from over her, my ears could hear all the chaotic screaming and yelling in the background. None of it mattered to me.

"Oh, my goodness, Jireh! What have you done?"

Smiling on the inside, I did what I wanted to do my whole life. I borrowed God's vengeance. I'm sure my pastor would not have wanted me to use Romans 12:19 in this way, but I decided in that moment that I would repent to my true Judge later.

♦

"Mel, put Jireh in the tub and get her dressed for church," Aunt Bert called upstairs from the kitchen.

"Yes ma'am!" my cousin, Melody, yelled down the stairs from her bedroom. Her room was directly across from mine in an old colonial, but majestic looking home. At least that's what I thought because at my age everything looked brand new to me now that I was no longer in that one-room apartment with my daddy. He took me to live with Aunt Bert because he was going into the military for a few years. At least, that's what he told me. I would later find out that the military was code for prison.

"Make sure you wash her good and brush all that wild hair of hers too," Aunt Bert said, continuing to bark orders like a drill sergeant.

Mel silently sucked her teeth. "Yes ma'am. Come on Ji-Ji. It's time for our favorite fun." I giggled at the thought of playing the electrocution game in the water at bath time. Melody Johns was Aunt Bert's youngest child from her first marriage. Aunt Bert had three in all, and her older two sons had already moved out with families of their own. Both were very wealthy and stayed as far away from Aunt Bert as much as they could. Melody was her only girl. She was 11 years old.

The only weird thing about her was she always dressed up or pretended to be a boy whenever Aunt Bert wasn't around. She would talk in slang and put socks in her pants. She would take Aunt Bert's eye makeup and draw black lines on her face to make her look like she had hair on her lip and chin. Whenever Aunt Bert would leave for church on Thursday night, she would pretend she and I were married. I thought that was very crazy, but she made it fun. Then she would play the electrocution game with me, most times in the tub, but whenever Aunt Bert went out of the house and left her to watch me, we would play in her room or the attic. I took off my Barbie nightgown and Strawberry Shortcake underwear and went into the bathroom. Mel came in and turned on the water. As I stood there naked, waiting for the tub to fill up, Mel just stared at me. She always did this. She began to play and pull on my long braids, and I laughed as she tickled my nose with the end of my braid. She always started our game the same way: "Ji-Ji, do you know what we are doing?" she asked.

"Yes Mel, we are playing the electrocution game again. Are you going to make my body feel a shock again?" I asked excitedly.

"Yes, Ji, you're going to feel the shock and so am I," she replied in a whisper. Now, I didn't know why I liked this game so much. Was it because Mel told me I was supposed to or because I was only five years old and was too afraid to tell Mel I didn't want to play, or was it simply because I really liked the shocking feeling I got all over when we played? The truth was, I used to think it was weird, and I always felt ashamed even though I didn't know why; something about it felt very wrong, but I was accustomed to feeling this so much that I began to find ways to have this feeling even when Mel wasn't around.

One thing I knew without Mel having to tell me was I better not tell Aunt Bert. I got into the tub that had so many bubbles I could have choked on them. Mel knew I liked the bubbles and would put extra bubbles in whenever she wanted to kiss me, and I didn't want her to. She would always say, "Ji-Ji, don't you want to get married one day? You can't get married unless you know how to kiss, so let me teach you. Then we can get electrocuted together. If you help me get electrocuted with you, I will put so many bubbles in the tub you will feel like you in the clouds with your Mommy."

Although I didn't like when she did it, the thought of the bubbles having the ability to allow me to see a woman I never met before excited and saddened me. I longed to see my mommy. I don't think I would have ever recognized her if I did see her, but in a strange way I missed her. Aunt Bert said she died doing the only good thing she offered the world, and that was having me. Come to think of it, that was probably the nicest thing Aunt Bert ever said to me.

Mel helped me to sit in the tub as she grabbed the Dove soap to wash me. She stared at me as she washed all over my tiny body. As she started her way down my tummy, she leaned in and kissed my forehead.

"I am going to make sure you are nice and clean for church today. Everyone is going to smell you and want to hug on you," said Mel. She put her hand down between my little skinny legs, soap still in hand. She took her other hand and rubbed the red dots on my chest and kissed my lips. I didn't like that part of the game. I just wanted her to hurry up and electrocute me so we could leave the bathroom. However, she took her time today and was acting a little crazier than normal. She took her shirt off and her little boobs were in my face. Suddenly, I wanted to get out of the tub.

"Mel, I don't want to play anymore," I said, tears welling up in my eyes. Mel looked at me like Freddie Kruger had taken over her body. She grabbed me by my hair and said, "Kiss my boobies right now. Lick on them like a dog licks up his water from a bowl!" she whispered in a creepy voice. I had never seen Mel like this when we played before. I was so afraid, but I couldn't get out of the tub. Reluctantly, I followed Mel's orders and put my little pink lips around the dark brown dot on her boobies and licked them.

"Good, now suck on it like a baby bottle," she said in the same creepy whisper, except now she was breathing heavily and rubbing the soap bar vigorously between my legs in my private area. I was burning. This wasn't something we ever did. In the past, Mel always touched my "shock spot" a few times until my legs shook and I would feel like a fish in the water. She told me that I was being electrocuted by her. She asked if I liked it but never waited for me to answer because she said I was supposed to like it. So, whenever she would ask, I would just say yes. I began to weep silently with my mouth still on her boob. I was too afraid to tell her to stop or call for Aunt Bert. So, I tried to think of something, anything that made me happy whenever I was sad. I blocked out all the things happening at that point as Mel pushed her fingers inside me and took her other hand and pushed those fingers inside her at the same time. I wanted to scream, cry, and yell, but all I could do was lay there halfway drowning in the tub and let her do whatever she wanted to do. She kept pushing, in and out and around like she was trying to find something. It hurt so badly, and it burned like the alcohol Aunt Bert used to clean my scrapes when I fell outside.

"Jesus, I don't know if you are a real person, but whoever you are that I am on my way to hear about, can you please make me disappear?"

That was the first time I ever prayed outside of praying over my food, before I went to bed, and "The Lord's Prayer" that was taught to me in Sunday School. I just wanted to die. I thought if I would just fall all the way into the water and drown myself, this nightmare would end. I knew if my hair got wet, Aunt Bert would beat Mel. I descended slowly down, but Mel must have figured out my plan because she roughly grabbed me by the middle of my hair, pinned my head back to the tub, placed her lips over mine, and darted her tongue in and out of my mouth while also jamming her fingers in and out of my vagina.

"Kiss me back, or I will do it harder. I am going to make you good at this!" Mel said with a fire in her eyes I had never seen. *How could this be happening?* Surely, Aunt Bert was wondering what is taking us so long. *Had time stopped? Where is God? Doesn't He see what is happening to me? Doesn't He care?* I cried and cried until my tears could have refilled the tub. I laid there, my private area on fire, my head and neck hurting, and my soul slowly dying. I went into the deepest parts of my mind for peace.

"*Blessed are the poor in spirit, for theirs is the kingdom of heaven. Blessed are they that mourn, for they shall be comforted. Blessed are the meek. Blessed are the meek. For they shall inherit the earth. Blessed are they who should hunger and thirst after righteousness for they shall be filled. Blessed....blessed. Blessed are the merciful for they shall obtain mercy.*" I sang in my head the first song I ever learned. Suddenly, with sweat all over her face and mine, Mel let out a deep groan into my mouth while breathing heavily. She stopped stabbing me with her fingers and fell back on the floor, into the corner of the door and wall. She began to weep quietly. I sat in the tub afraid to make a move or a sound. As Mel peeled herself off the floor in what looked like total shame on her face, she grabbed the towel off the sink and threw it on the floor next to the tub.

"Dry off," she said dryly and walked out. I sat there in a fog. My mind was totally void of all thoughts. As I tried to get up out of the tub, my legs violently shook, and some of my hair stuck lifelessly to the back of the tub. I felt my head to find two bald spots. As the tears fell down my face, I got out of the tub to dry off with the shamefully thrown towel on the floor, with not a bubble in sight.

She never talked to me after I came out of the bathroom. She didn't even help me get dressed. In fact, she seemed disgusted by me. I was so confused. When she finally came in my room, she grabbed the hairbrush, quickly took my braids out, and attempted to put it into a ponytail. She paused briefly when she brushed the middle of my very fine but wavy hair, probably noticing the bald spots from where she pulled my hair out earlier in the bathroom. I could hear her sniffling with each brush stroke. She finally accomplished the mission of putting a ponytail in my hair before swiftly walking out of my room. While at church, I sat quietly in the second row with the rest of the children's choir members, reliving the dreadful memories that were sure to haunt me for years to come. What did I know? I was five years old; I didn't even know how to spell rape or molestation, let alone tell someone about it. I sat in the pew and thought, "God, please help me!" He was the only one I could tell, anyway. Across the room, Mel sat next to some of her friends from church. I turned around and looked her way. When she noticed, she quickly put her head down. Guilt covered her face as she lowered her shame-filled eyes. I knew she knew she was wrong, and I had no clue how to react now. That was the last interaction we had that day. She went out of her way to avoid me, only speaking to me when she was forced to. Aunt Bert noticed that the once inseparable duo, "Frick and Frack," as she not-so affectionately called us, were more like Superman and kryptonite now.

"What's wrong with y'all?" she asked. Almost in perfect unison, we both mumbled, "nothing." She noticed we both went right to our rooms and closed the door. She even asked if we both wanted ice cream before bedtime, but she got nothing but silence. Now, any adult, I would think, would have enough sense to know something happened from the morning before church until the evening when returning home. If she had come into my room, I probably would have had the strength to tell her. However, she didn't come into my room. She didn't come in and rescue me from my sorrow. She didn't come in to comfort me in any way. My nightmare was just beginning, and it was only going to get worse. Without knocking but as silent as she could be, Mel came in with rage all over her face, walked right in front of my face as I sat on my bed in fear, and slapped me.

"If you ever think about telling anyone, I will kill you and send you to your dead mother!" she hissed at me. Our relationship was non-existent after that moment. I did my best to stay away from Mel. Aunt Bert, noticing this drastic change, never said a word.

♦

I walked out to the front of the house, conflicted but satisfied at the same time.

Ji, why did you do that? I asked myself as I stood there in the grass, leaning against the great oak tree, thinking of the whole kitchen fiasco. I took off my sneakers and rubbed my toes through the warm southern grass. Years of counseling and I still allowed this woman to get under my skin. Being around her for any amount of time was always sickening for me but having to stomach a family reunion with people who never really treated me like family made my skin crawl. What made it worse was in our "family", everyone was in the other's business constantly, so there was always something reality show-worthy.

I could still hear all the dramatics coming from the great room from the oak tree. Running my fingers over the bark, I noticed a BMW X5 coming up the road and into the crescent-shaped driveway. It had been five years since I had seen Mel, but here she was, ready to perform. We never spoke of the incident since that day, but I relived it every day since. I endured so many tragedies because of that day. I continued to stand under the tree, watching Mel have small, loving interactions with family members as she walked up the grand marble stairs. Then I noticed a quick mood shift, packed with fast-talking and complete with animated tales I couldn't hear, and suddenly, Mel rushed into the house.

"Here we go," I thought to myself. However, this time, I was ready. It was long overdue for resolutions and truth. I put my sneakers back on just in time to see Mel on the large wrap-around porch surveying the yard, with a half bloody rag in her hand.

"I'm right here. You do not have to look for me, Mel. I am not running anymore!" I said with a strength she was unfamiliar with. I found my voice at that moment. Counseling with no resolve was getting me nowhere, and this was my moment to bury the skeletons I carried with me since that dreadful day in the tub. As Mel walked towards me in the yard, fist balled up and rage on her face, I threw my hair up into a tight ponytail, ready for the fight, and hopefully some resolution and peace.

Let's go.

Angell Hodges-Morris

About Angell Hodges-Morris

Angell Morris, native of Connecticut, currently resides in Delaware. She believes in Christ, is a wife and mother of three, and owns two food businesses, Signatures Soul & Sea and Signatures By Angell Catering, LLC. Angell Strives to live an encouraging life and push all in her circle of influence to their greatness.

"How do you ask for forgiveness when you don't know you've wounded someone?"

Donyell M. Bruce Coleman, "Forgiveness and the Wounded Child" ♦ *V1*

THE WOUNDED CHILD

Jordan Taylor

Sleeping peacefully. It all started while I was simply sleeping peacefully. I opened my eyes, awakened by the sounds of moans, and what I saw shocked me. It was *him*, masturbating at my bedside as he watched me sleep peacefully. I didn't make a sound. I couldn't. I was in shock! *What was he thinking?*

It was at that moment that he pulled my shorts and panties to the side and forced himself onto me. I was 14, and he was my mother's boyfriend.

What was happening? WHAT IS HAPPENING TO ME!? He continued to ram his penis inside of me, and there I laid, crying, tears rolling down my face so much so that I could feel the puddles forming in my ears and rolling out on to my pillows. He continued for what felt like forever, and when he pulled out, he came all over my shorts. He left the room and shut the door and I laid there, still in shock.

What just happened to me? WHAT JUST HAPPENED TO ME? WHY!? I didn't sleep that night; instead, I cried while my mother laid sound asleep in the room right around the corner. Little did I know, that would just be night number one.

Mom

My mother was a single mother–a hard-working woman, and she worked long hours. I would cook and clean for the entire household and was used to being around my mother's boyfriend. He was younger than my mother, much younger than her, about 23 years old. In fact, he dated a friend of mine (who was about 6 years older than me) who praise danced with me at church. Church was where we met him. He was fun! Could sing his behind off and we got along great. I was used to him dating my friend and considered him a friend although we didn't hang out, just talked at church. Church is where we spent most of our time outside of school and work. I praise danced and sang in the choir. My mother also sang in the choir and participated in weekly Bible study. We were at church many days out of the week, and when I wasn't at church, I spent a lot of time at my grandmother's house. I often called her mom. She cooked for me, and we always went shopping! That was my girl!

Isaiah

During the 7th grade, I met a boy, Isaiah, who was my grandmother's neighbor. We became the best of friends and started spending a lot of time together. Two years later, my first year of high school, we started dating, and I was head over heels. I hadn't had many boyfriends, but Isaiah made me so happy! He was so sweet, so kind, and very protective of me. I loved everything about him.

Now, my family wasn't too fond of him. After all, he was four years older than me, but what they didn't know was that I lied to him about my age. I spent a lot of time with him, but once my family found out we were dating, we had to sneak around. One year, my mother called him out and told him we couldn't be friends any longer. He was heartbroken, but fate would not have us be separated for too long. Sometime later, my mother began letting him visit me at home. I stopped going to my grandma's house after school and started catching the school bus home. He and I went to separate schools, but after school, he would meet me at my house, close to the time that my mom got off. My mom trusted that were being responsible, and we were.

Him

Now back to who we will refer to as "him." Shortly after my mom started dating him, he moved in. I wasn't surprised, as this was typical behavior of my mom. I didn't know why she was like that, but I was a child. Who was I to ask questions? What I didn't like was having to clean up after the grown men she brought into the house. It was cool at first, but then my mom didn't like having Isaiah over. She would claim that my boyfriend was too disrespectful to her, but that's not what I remembered. To this day, I believe that her new boyfriend had a lot to do with her change of heart. So, there again, we snuck around. We spent time at the movies, parks, other family members' houses, and back to grandma's I went. I hated being at home knowing that he played a role in my mother's judgment. Couldn't she see Isaiah loved me? He would never let anything bad happen to me; he was so kind, sweet, and had the utmost respect for me. He was the total opposite of what I had seen my mother put up with.

Quilla

Quilla was a friend who I met freshman year of high school. That was my girl; she was sweet as could be but straight hood! She was completely misunderstood and lived a rough life. Her mother, like mine, put men before her. She spent a lot of time at my house, and my mom ended up taking her in after she got kicked out of her house because she confronted her mom about her stepfather. Little did we know her mother would never check on her again. We became the best of friends. We shared the same major at our vo-tech high school, which was cosmetology. *Cosmo girls for life!* She kept her hair laid and mine too! She could dance her behind off, but me, not so much. I was more of a ballet style dancer. Hip hop was not my thing! You could catch us at school during the week and at a party on the weekends! We were just two teens having fun.

Him

The next morning after he forced himself on to me, I avoided him like the plague. I walked to the bus stop like nothing ever happened. After school, I met Isaiah in the square. It was a central location where all the public buses met to pick up riders. This became our meeting place. I didn't tell Isaiah what had happened. I smiled and laughed as if nothing ever occurred. After all, I grappled within myself for not saying "stop" or "don't," and last night was obviously my fault.

I caught the last bus of the night home and greeted everyone when I got in like any normal day. Days went by and I repeated the same steps: wake up, avoid him, walk to the bus stop, go to school, meet Isaiah after school, catch the last bus home and greet everybody like normal. The following week came, and that night, Isaiah and I did not meet. After all, we had been sneaking around, and I did not want to get caught. Technically, my mom didn't say I couldn't talk to Isaiah. She just didn't want him in her house anymore, but she also wouldn't have wanted me sneaking to hang with him. I just didn't want her to tell me to stop talking to Isaiah. So, I caught the bus home, and when I got there, there *he* was, sitting in the living room. I felt like he was waiting for me.

I walked in the house and began doing the dishes because I did not want to hear my mother's mouth when she got off work. Then it happened; I felt his hand rubbing my behind and heading around towards my vagina. I could not believe this was happening again!

I shouted his name this time and said, "What are you doing!?"

He asked me, "Don't you like it?"

I quickly responded, "No!" and told him I was going to tell my mother that he was touching on me.

He told me "Go ahead. I'll let her know that you came on to me."

"But that's not true!"

"Who do you think she'll believe?" he asked me.

At that moment, I knew he had the upper hand. Like I said before, my mother had a habit of putting men before me, so why would this time be any different? He then dropped his pants and told me to do what I was supposed to do if I didn't want him telling my mom that I came on to him. And then it happened all over again. This went on for months–five, to be exact. He forced himself on to me a total of 11 times. It didn't matter when or where I was; I could be downstairs on the couch watching TV and my mom upstairs lying in bed or knocked out like a light. I could be just walking in from school and my mom on her way home–it didn't matter!

I needed a way out, so I got a job working as a volunteer at a local hospital in the records department. I loved it! It kept me busy after school. Shortly after getting the gig, my best friend, Quilla, moved in. I was so happy I was busy after school and then had company when I got home, so I wasn't alone with him. Still, no one knew what I had been through. No one; not Quilla or Isaiah, but it finally stopped. I felt relieved, but not free. I had a feeling of guilt, like this was all my fault. *Why did I let this happen to me for so long?* I allowed this to go on for months!

One day, while on my break at the hospital, I got a call from Quilla. I answered, and all I heard was shrieking screams and cries that turned my stomach. She didn't have to utter a word because at that moment, I already knew what happened. He had done the same thing to her. I immediately left work and caught the public transportation home. When I got there, she was still crying uncontrollably, and he was gone. We shared a room and had two separate beds. She told me exactly how it happened, and you wouldn't believe that her story was the same as mine; she was napping and was awakened by his moans. This was night number one all over again. It was at that point that I finally shared what had been going on for months with me and him. We cried together, and we vowed never to leave each other alone. We started going everywhere together. When I would go to the local hospital after school, she would go to a cousin of mine's house down the street until

I was done, and then we would catch the bus home. When I went to church for dance, she would come and wait for me. When I had to cheer at games after school, you would see her at all the games with me, and when I would sneak to see Isaiah, she would be there too. I believe it was our new pattern that protected us from him because he never attempted to do anything to me or Quilla once things changed. Who knew that we had to be this strategic at 14?

The Neighborhood Church

While it's true that we kept smiles on our faces and walked around carrying each other's secret like nothing ever happened, the reality was that we were broken, truly broken, by these events.

One Sunday morning, we woke up early for no reason in particular, and I said, "Hey Quillz,"–that's what I called her–"Let's go to the church around the corner." So, we did. I don't recall what was so compelling about the sermon that day, and to be honest I don't think it had anything to do with what we were going through, but we both cried and cried and cried from the start of praise and worship to the call to offering. Once the sermon was over, we walked home from church, and both said, "We have to say something."

That evening, my mom sat in the dining room after she finished cooking while Quilla and I sat in my room upstairs. Without thinking, I called my stepmom (she and my dad weren't truly married but they had been together for many years) and told her everything from start to finish, leaving nothing out. By the end of the call, she cried and said, "You know you have to tell your mom, right?" I was so frustrated! I called her because I needed advice, but that was not the advice that I wanted to hear, though the release of telling my stepmom felt so good.

I told her I couldn't, and she replied, "If you don't tell your mother, then I will have to tell your father." I feared my father would go to jail for killing him, so in haste, the next steps I took I truly thought would stop everything–stop me from feeling guilty, stop my dad from killing him, and make the pain all go away.

The Truth

It was time. After we got off the phone with my stepmom, we knew we had no other choice but to tell my mom. Apprehensively, we walked downstairs, and I did all the talking. I told my mother that we had both been molested by him. We never got the chance to give details. In fact, we immediately felt stupid for coming to her. The look on her face was emotionless, cold, and distant. She didn't say *anything. Nothing at all.* We all sat there in silence until Quilla and I left the table and went to sit on the steps outside. It was dark, and we were getting eaten up by mosquitos, but we still sat outside for hours. The feeling of guilt was still there for me, but how could it be when I finally told the truth?

Finally, he came home. We were still sitting outside on the steps, and he said "what's up" to us like any other normal day and we just nodded. We both surely knew tonight would be the night that my mother would let him have it, kick him out, and call the police. Little did I know he would talk his way right out of this one.

He told her we were both lying. Every single thing we said was a lie. Around 2 a.m., Quilla and I went back in the house. By this time, he and my mother were in their bedroom, door closed, and we went into our room and closed the door. We were so confused. *Why wasn't he gone? Why wasn't there any yelling? Why wasn't my mother in our room consoling us?* The next morning came, and we didn't go to school. Instead, we were greeted by a crowd: my aunt, uncle, dad, and stepmom. They were coming to our rescue. I thought they would come guns blazing but I'm sure no one wanted to go to jail that day. He was already gone when the cops were called. They came and placed me and Quilla in the back of the car and got our statements. That was it! My mom was still speechless, cold, and distant. In fact, she argued with my family for even showing up at her house. She was very defensive. She didn't care about what me and Quilla just told her. She was more interested in getting people away from her house. Quilla and I packed a bag and left with my dad.

The Transition

The next few weeks were unexplainable. I wasn't used to staying with my dad. He really hadn't been in my life much, but I knew that he loved me, and he came when I needed him the most. He was my protector. He made sure to purchase all the things that I needed to feel comfortable. He went out and bought me a new bed and allowed me to decorate my room the way I wanted. We painted it, added a seating area, and bought a new TV. These things made me feel great, and it was a refreshing feeling, being away from the chaos that I had previously experienced. Quilla and I enjoyed being waited on and not preyed upon. Everything was different. The only concern that we had at the time of moving in with Dad was the distance from our school. He lived about an hour away from our school, but there was a school bus that came his way. Because of the distance, it was also difficult for me to see Isaiah. I knew I couldn't stay very long, but where would I go? I certainly wasn't thinking about going back home with my mother–that was a hard no. Though I rarely saw Isaiah, everything was going great with my dad until one day he called me into his room and said that he wanted to talk with me. He told me that although everything was going great, he could no longer take care of Quilla, and that she had to go back home. At that moment, my heart sank. Quilla was my best friend, and I knew she would not be welcomed back in her home. I also knew that she needed me right now more than ever. How could I tell her this? I understood my father's viewpoint, but it just wasn't fair. That night, I talked to Quilla and explained she could no longer stay with us. She told me with her mouth that she understood, but her body language said something different. We cried together, both trying to figure out the next move. He gave her a week to leave the house. During that time, she went to social services and told them she had nowhere to go. What happened to Quilla would haunt me for the rest of my life. I stayed with my dad for the remainder of my sophomore year and the beginning of my junior year before moving out.

Kim & Booter

Remember when I told you a group of people came to my rescue the day after I told my mother what happened? My Aunt Kim and Uncle Booter were there front and center. They yelled at my mother about how wrong she was. They told me that day that they would take me in, but the caveat was that I could not bring Quilla because they couldn't take care of both of us. For that reason, I declined their offer. Who knew that life would have me sitting on the bed sharing a room with my little cousin several months later? By this time, I was in my junior year of high school.

My aunt and uncle were the best; they made sure that I had everything that I needed. Supposedly, they received a call from my dad who asked how he could help, but he never did. My mother, on the other hand, never even reached out. I hadn't spoken to her in over a year.

I enjoyed staying with my aunt and uncle. They cooked every night–good food too! My aunt stayed on me about my homework and stressed how important these final years of high school were. She helped me with homework when I let it get the best of me, and she was as passionate about me as she was about her stepchildren. She was nurturing, and I looked up to her. This experience was nothing like what I was used to. Living with my aunt and uncle meant I was closer to school, and closer to Isaiah. We began hanging out again, but before I knew it, I got pregnant. Who would have thought I would be 16 and pregnant? When I told my aunt and uncle, I was prepared to be told that I had to leave, but no–it was the total opposite. Though me being pregnant wasn't the course that they wanted for my life, they embraced it and became even more nurturing. Although I was furious with my mother, everything in me told me I had to tell her. My aunt filled my mom's shoes wonderfully, but I was yearning for the love that I was missing from her. There was nothing like having my own mom experience this time with me. So, I called her.

Isaiah

While staying at my dad's, I never told Isaiah what happened. I never even asked him why he thought I moved. I kept this secret to myself for over a decade. I was embarrassed and upset and the last thing I needed was sympathy. I wanted to put everything behind me. We began meeting up again like old times, hanging out, going to dinner, checking out the movies. He made me laugh, and he filled my heart with so much joy. In the moments we shared, he took all the pain away. When I got pregnant, I was unsure of how to feel. We only had sex a few times. I guess that didn't matter. For him, this meant that it was time to grow up. For me, it meant that I needed to find a place to stay.

Once I called my mother to tell her I was pregnant, she smiled through the phone. She was ecstatic! She wanted me to move back home, and she told me she would kick *him* out. It was the end of senior year, and I missed my mom, so without hesitation, I moved back home. Like she promised, he was already gone by the time I got there. I had our daughter at 17, two months before graduation. Then two weeks later, Isaiah would be found in the middle of the street, shot, and fighting for his life. Who knew that this would all be happening to me? Although I was back home living with my mother, I became even more depressed. I lost my best friend to the system and cycle of homelessness, the father of my child was in a coma fighting for his life, and I was living in the home where the demons kept reminding me of the past.

Quilla

Remember when I told you that what happened to Quilla would haunt me for the rest of my life? Well, when Quilla had to leave my dad's house, she ended up in a group home. We barely spoke after that because she had no cell phone. Some days, I wouldn't even be able to find her; she stopped coming to school, and it crushed me. She was my best friend, and this was all my fault. Had we not said anything to my mom, Quilla and I would still be living in the house, protecting each other, and continuing to go to school together. Quilla eventually had three beautiful children, but our friendship would change forever. We still didn't talk much, and when I could find her, she would either be in a shelter or living with friends. It pained me as I got older.

When I turned 18, I got my own apartment, and by then I had a 2-year-old. I somehow got a hold of Quilla through social media, and she told me she was pregnant with her first child and staying at a shelter. I could not believe it; I needed to get her out of there, so I drove all the way to Germantown, Pennsylvania and got my friend from the shelter. She stayed with me for about two years until one day she moved out, and years later, I found her in another shelter. I could only believe that Quilla's life was turning out that way because of me.

Fast Forward

My life didn't turn out so bad; I brought my first house at 19 and was living the "American Dream." Yes, Isaiah survived, after being in the hospital for three months and undergoing over 25 surgeries causing him to become disabled. A few years later, I got pregnant with my and Isaiah's second child, and we named her Riley.

One year, for my birthday, my mom wanted to take me to D.C. to

19the African American History Museum followed by a dinner. I was excited. I packed bags for me, Isaiah, who was now my husband, and my daughters, Chloe and Riley. I booked a hotel, and I even invited my sister-in-law. I was so excited to be going away. My mother was known for being short tempered and snappy and for some reason today was one of those days. Throughout the tour of the museum, she made a few smart comments and set the tone for me not wanting to be in her presence. During the tour, one-and-a-half-year-old Riley walked with my mother while I pushed the empty stroller. After the tour, my husband and I went to the gift shop, because we truly enjoyed the museum and wanted a few souvenirs. Whenever we went away, we always bought books for the kids and this time was no different, but we were having trouble deciding on which book to get, so we were taking a long time. My mom, who was waiting outside with Riley, my sisters, my sister's friend, and her mother were growing inpatient, the museum was closing, and we were trying our best to hurry.

Before we knew it, my mother began walking away and headed towards the parking garage. About five minutes after she left, we left the gift shop, and I realized that I still had the stroller but no baby. I didn't think much of it. After all, we were parked in the same garage. Once we got to the garage, I called my mother to find out where she was, because I needed to get Riley or give my mother Riley's car seat. When my mother answered the phone, she was already on the road, driving in DC where traffic and drivers were known to be crazy, and the restaurant was 45 mins away. I asked her to turn back so that I could give her the car seat or so that Riley could ride with me. She told me no, and at that moment the fire lit inside of me! Who was she to tell me no, and that she wasn't turning around with my child? How could she take a 45-minute drive with my one-year-old without a car seat? I paced back and forth helplessly because my mother was nowhere nearby. I told everyone riding with me that I would drive to the restaurant and would come back for them. my mind filled with so much rage, and I had every intention of going to the restaurant, getting my baby, and fighting my mom like a broad on the street. I began having flashbacks to when my mom didn't protect me and now, she wasn't protecting my child. What kind of person was she!?

Right before I hopped into the driver's seat, my mom called my husband's phone asking where we were because she was close, and I became calm. I told myself that my baby was almost near and that staying calm was best. I had it in my mind not to say anything to my mother when she came and to just grab my children, but as soon as I opened the backseat to the car once she pulled up, my mom fixed her lips to say, "And you better not ever talk to me the way you were on the phone."

That was it. I couldn't contain myself. She had the audacity to tell me how to speak to her when she just drove for over 20 minutes with my daughter not in a car seat. At that moment, I blacked out. This lady, who didn't care about the wellbeing of me or my child had the nerve to fix her lips and say something other than sorry.

My mouth spoke before I could think, and I said, "If you weren't my mom, I would punch you dead in your motherfucking face."

She responded, "Well, do it." I walked towards the front of her car so fast until my husband grabbed me. He swooped me up and told me to get the kids and come on. For months, I would go without speaking to my mother again. My children were not allowed to go to her house, and why would they? She couldn't protect them if any harm came their way.

Therapy

After D.C., I went back to my therapist, who I was seeing for depression and anxiety, in addition to another therapist for the sexual assault. I thought I was making progress, but the incident in D.C. forced me to believe that this was not the case. I was filled with self-blame, hatred, anger, helplessness, and sadness. I made yet another appointment and sat in the chair, expressing my feelings yet again about my mother and what she did to me several years ago. There I was questioning *how could she choose a man over me? How could she not protect my children? Why would she want to bring harm to them like she did me? Was I not good enough? Did my life or that of my children mean nothing to her?* I sat in the chair thinking out loud, asking all these rhetorical questions as my therapist watched me weep.

With the advice of my therapist, I decided I needed to have a conversation with my mother. I tried for months until she finally agreed to speak with me. I knew that the only reason she chose to speak with me was because I would not let her see my children. But this break was necessary. It was a choice that I had to make to protect my children.

She agreed to meet me, so I picked the place–the library. I didn't want to hear any yelling, and I most certainly did not want to get into a physical altercation with my mother. We sat at a table near a window, and I told her how I felt about him and how I felt about the incident in D.C. Yet again, my mother sat there cold as ice. She barely uttered a word. All she wanted to know was when she could see her grandkids.

It took multiple sessions with my mom for her to truly understand the capacity of how that situation with him haunted me to this day, how my fear for the safety of my children was a *real* fear, and how her reaction changed my life forever, until one day she finally broke down. She told me that she, too, was molested by a close family member and that she never told her mother. She was never protected, and in fact, this person stayed in the family all her life. It was at that moment that I knew my mother wasn't equipped with the right tools to give me what I needed, what I yearned for, or what I desired as a response to my assault. How could she? No one ever did that for her.

Having that final conversation with my mother changed my viewpoint. I decided to forgive my mother but make no mistake–I could never forget. To this day, I have not forgiven him for what he did to me. He altered my childhood in a way that cannot be undone. I haven't seen him since the day I left my mother's house, but I know he could never be worth my freedom or my dignity. If I ever saw him, I would walk right past him with my head held high. Although my story is not complete, and I have not forgiven my abuser or myself, my prayer is that this will be accomplished through time and continued aggressive therapy. I have faith that my love life will improve with my husband, my friendship with Quilla will come back together, my relationship with my mother will continue to grow, my appreciation for my father will stay the same, and my love for my aunt and uncle will forever be with me.

I'm sure at this point, you were looking for a happy ending, but sadly, I am still on my journey. Although my story doesn't have a fairytale resolution, in time, this pain that I am experiencing will fade away and I will be able to forgive him and myself for what happened to me at the age of 14.

Jordan Taylor

About Jordan Taylor

Jordan Brittney Taylor–daughter, wife, mother, sister, granddaughter, cousin, friend. Jordan was born and raised in Wilmington, Delaware. She became a mother at 16. but did not let that stop her from breaking barriers in life. She is a graduate of Howard High School and proudly holds a B.A. in Organizational Dynamics with a minor in Human Resource Management from Wilmington University. Jordan became the first one in her family to obtain her college degree. She is now on the journey of pursuing her master's degree. Jordan became a homeowner at 19 and purchased her first rental property at 27. Although Jordan has had many struggles, they have turned out to be her greatest lessons. Jordan has a passion for crafting and entrepreneurship. Along with her rental property, which is paid in full, she developed an all-natural Loc & Twist Gel for natural hair, a Hair & Body Oil, and she also has a T-shirt business. Jordan believes she is becoming the best version of herself because she is growing smarter, wiser, and more enlightened. She is evolving and loves it! She spends quality time with family and friends and the loves of her life! Jordan has been with her husband Isaiah for seventeen years and they have been married for seven years. They are the proud parents of Chloe, Riley, and Garrison. Jordan has accomplished all of this while battling mental illness and many health issues, but she never gives up! Her daily mantra is the Serenity Prayer: *"God, grant me the serenity to accept the things I cannot change, the courage to change the things I can, and the wisdom to know the difference."*

"Little prayer, little power. Much prayer, much power."

Charlotte Miller-Lacy, "We Rise Above" ♦ *V1*

"NOS" AND "CLOSED DOORS" ARE GOD'S PROTECTION

Tangie Samuels

June 1, 2021, #12yearsandcounting. Yep, 12 years in corporate America when I just knew I'd be gone by now but.... God had other plans.

After having my now 17-year-old son, DuPont decided to "let go" of their contractors, and my lateral move from URS Corp from New York to Delaware was all done and over with, ending an 8-year good run. What was I going to do now? Since 2002, I had been trying to get into Christiana Care with some type of admin job, but God had other plans. It was time to start temping because I wasn't doing any fast-food services since my family had grown. I had given up my "independence," as my dad said back then, and started a new life. There was no way I was about to become dependent on a man I barely knew... oh yeah, I wanted to avoid all of that.

The banking capital of the world was hiring on a temp-to-hire basis, and I was going to take it, but I quickly realized I had to think about this one. I reminded myself, *You have your child and little sister, and you want to work nights? Then you'll have to leave them with your fiancée. Girl, you're still getting to know him!* But what other way was there? None!

I was interviewed, hired, and began in customer service. I made money, had the bomb schedule, and I was happier than a pig in mud. Seven years later, in 2009, I'd be a part of yet another large company's layoff. Man, all my life I'd heard about layoffs but was never a part of one, especially not including thousands of people. *Who the-? What the-? Is this what they do in Delaware*? I couldn't keep doing this, but God had other plans.

I was back to the drawing board with the temp agency. Why the temp agency, you asked? Good question. So, being born and raised in New York City, I watched my folks that never "continued" their education bust their butts working for temp agencies, as this was the way to keep a job. Plus, you got paid weekly and always had money. Hustle hard, play hard, and never depend on anyone else to get you where you need to be. Plus, I still had three other mouths to feed.

I landed another temp-to-hire gig with Barclays Bank on January 1, 2009. This was a ride I didn't prepare for, but I had plans to do what I needed to do to work hard, keep this job, and get hired. I asked all the questions about their stability and made sure I did my research. I was getting older, and I didn't want to lose another job. The uncertainty and instability didn't feel good, especially because I had no control over anything.

Talk about starting from the bottom; I had to work two late nights until 9 p.m. and a weekend day…ugh. On top of that, I had to drive into Wilmington every single day. You know, being from Brooklyn, New York, I never had to drive. I missed my trains and buses that ran all day, every day. Yes, Delaware has them, but they don't run as frequently, and I had to do so much transferring… no thank you.

In June 2009, I was hired permanently. It wasn't my dream job, but it was permanent. Collecting money from folks didn't feel good, and boy, folks knew how to pull on your heart strings when they were behind. I had goals and numbers to meet, and this job was stressful, but the money was good. Going home and trying to discuss what happened at work or even sharing stories was a bit draining mentally. My husband reminded me I didn't know those folks, and that there was nothing I could do for them. He also reminded me I needed to leave those feelings at work so that once I was home, I could be mentally and physically there for my family. I learned quickly not to bring "work" home and began checking my day at the door when it was over. I prayed things would change and maybe, just maybe, something would come through that was closer to home.

Ok God, I see you. They bought a building in Newark, literally 10 minutes from my house and the call center was going to be the first department in the building. I love it. There was room for growth, more money, and stability–all the things I'd been praying for.

In the following five years, I applied for five different JEPs (job enrichment positions) that I just knew would turn into a "new" position. I would get so upset after working in these departments for three to six months because there would be no movement upward. I questioned God: *Why not? I'm qualified. I learned these roles in and out. They liked me; they gave me more responsibility. I even earned extra incentive during these opportunities, so why not me?* Those no's were hard to take, but GOD. Let me tell you how, for every no I received from all five departments, those roles/departments were either merged and folks lost their jobs, or they were offered demotions, including salary decreases. I mean, from the top down, those folks that laughed at me behind my back but gave me the "at a girl" pats on the back, all while denying me opportunities, were now sitting back in the same row with me. I quietly smiled every time someone came back but kept my thoughts to myself.

I realized then that God had me. Can you say grateful? I went through two more lay-off rounds, untouched and still employed. Wow! Amazed at what he did for little oh me, I still wasn't satisfied, definitely wasn't comfortable, and wouldn't take my shoes off to get comfortable because it seemed too good to be true.

On March 5, 2019, after being off for three months, I returned to work to a message about yet another lay off, which would be number five. *What?!* This was ridiculous, and it was happening as of December 2019. So, here we go again! I threw my hands up and basically gave up, giving my situation to the Lord and allowing him to do what he saw fit. Not only was I getting laid off, but now I had to travel back to Wilmington every day for work until then. *Why me?*

On December 2, our new department lead visited the office with the "new folks that were taking my job and asked me to train them. *Who? What? Train for what, my job? Hmmm. Yeah, sure, I'll slow grind this and show them very little… just the basics for sure, never all my tricks and work-a rounds.* On December 15, I was asked to extend my time, which included some additional severance money and they wanted me to travel to train the "other new folks." *I sure will. I'm not losing anything, and I will not be in the job pool with everyone else, this'll give me a chance at a better job after everyone else has left and hopefully find another job*… but God had other plans.

My last day was set for March 31, 2020. On March 16, I was supposed to fly out for two weeks and turn my equipment in while in Nevada. Covid changed all of that. My role was extended, yet again… but GOD! This time, the job was extended until June 30… *was this real?* Folks were texting me with questions about my extension, telling me how they were going to "do me dirty and I should've left with them." When I responded with "God's got me," without any back and forth–no "I'll figure it out… I'll be ok…" nothing–they all left me alone.

Fast forward to June 28, 2020. I was offered a team manager position because they were bringing the call center back to Delaware. I had recently begun applying for a few positions outside of the bank, but nothing panned out, so I stayed where I was. This offer was proof that I deserved to be where I was and proof that all my hard work was finally paying off. I finally got confirmation that the encouraging words that my Assistant Vice Presidents Kevin and Ashley shared with me were true. In the past, I'd taken the leap and shared my frustrations about feeling like I was continuously passed over for positions at work. I explained how I felt, told them I felt like banking, especially collections, wasn't for me. I was encouraged to apply for different positions within the bank, some of which I would later be offered.

This past year and a half has not been easy. I found myself, yet again, listening to folks talk about their struggles, their loss of family and friends, their unemployment issues and concerns, and here I was bringing work home again. The hardest part was hearing people say things like, "You're lucky to still have a job," or "Are you blind?" and even "Do you not know what's going on in the world?" I struggled and yet again, questioned where I was. *Why me?*

Then it hit me; I am living proof that praying, listening, and only moving when God tells you actually works. My mind was made up, though. I just knew I was leaving the bank, and I would not continue getting passed over or was I going to sit and wait for them to see me. I was leaving this bank, but… God has other plans.

Tangie Samuels

About Tangie Samuels

Tangie Samuels is a native of Brooklyn, NY. She is a mother of three, a wife of nearly 19 years, and a grandmother of four. She's been a Delawarean for over 20 years, thanks to her husband, Devin. Tangie is a people person and attracts folks everywhere she goes. You can often find her volunteering in the community and throughout Pennsylvania, New Jersey, and Maryland. Her dedication to serving others, mentoring and spreading the love she's soaked up in her life, gives her great joy and motivates her to keep serving. She loves dancing, singing, listening to music, writing, event planning and traveling. Tangie's life lessons have taught her to live for today. "Live, Love, and Laugh" is her everyday motto. She prides herself on knowing that there's a "*But God*" at the end of every situation.

"The rear view mirror is smaller for a reason. It's there only to give you a glimpse of your past and where you have traveled from"

Ursula McCoy, "Driving the Pickle Bus on a Guilt Trip" ♦ *V1*

VICTORIOUS

Latricia Pipkin

When you're feeling like a failure,

remember the grenades you have crushed,

The setbacks you have overcome,

And the battles you have won.

This journey through life is rough, I know,

but still with courage, you climb.

This strength you have built will take you places.

Be proud of the warrior you have become.

---Tene Edwards, *Walk with Wings*

Today, I feel blessed to see another day, but at the same time, as I sit here and talk about a dark time in my life that by God's grace, I overcame, I feel so many emotions. I know that this was God's plan for me even though writing my story wasn't something I ever imagined for myself. I just wanted to find a way to help a beautiful queen that may be going through a dark time in their lives know that with God, you can walk into victory and become victorious.

I'm also writing this for myself as well. I know that through all of this, God will continue to heal and strengthen me even more than he has at this point in my life. There is still trauma that I am working through, but I have overcome the fear of facing it head on so that I can become the woman that God would have for me to be, not the woman that I *want* to be.

This morning as I took my youngest child to school, I was listening to "He's A Wonder" by Israel Houghton and New Breed and tears rolled down my cheeks because my heart was heavy; however, I knew that no matter what I was going through, God was going to turn it around for my good just like he turned me from an addict to an overcomer. I must remind myself that when I feel that heaviness that, in the name of Jesus, I have the victory. God has truly done more for me than I really deserve. *God saved my life.*

My mom brought my older sister, brother, and me up in church and taught us the Bible. As I got older, I strayed from church because church took up one of my days on the weekend and I felt as a child that I was forced to go not realizing that my mom was bringing her children up in the way that God had directed her to and to be an example of a child of God. When I became old enough to decide to go to church for myself, I would go occasionally but only on special occasions or holidays, and then barely a handful of times during the year, and eventually, I stopped going all together. At that point, I chose to give up and walk away from God, not knowing that he would be the only one I would end up needing to turn to for help.

During the time I gave up on God, as well as myself, I fell into addiction. I was addicted to heroin for about three years. Heroin is a demon that will make everything seem better, and while you are caught up in it, it will snatch everything from your life. It will break you down, and it will ruin every relationship you have with every person in your life. It will cause you to distance yourself from everyone you love and make you want to be alone with nothing but the drug. This demon will weaken you and cause you to do things that you would never do if you weren't under its control.

Everything I was taught in church growing up, I chose to forget about because I wanted to go out with my so-called friends at the time to clubs and bars because I didn't want to miss what I thought was an enjoyable time. I didn't realize I wanted to be in that scene to mask the hurt, pain, and heartbreak that I was feeling. This would be the beginning of my dangerous walk down a dark path.

I never imagined that I would end up addicted to a drug because growing up, my dad was an addict and I got to see what it did to his life and how it affected my mom, my sister, my brother, and me. I always told myself growing up, I would never do the things in my life and to my life like he did. Little did I know I would end up treading down that same lonely road.

I went through postpartum depression and anxiety after I had my second and my third child. After my doctor diagnosed me with anxiety and depression, I was put on anti-depressants, which one of them was a narcotic. I was not only dealing with depression and anxiety, I also went through infidelity in my relationship around each of my three pregnancies, I masked all that pain until I was fed up and snapped. I went to the woman's apartment he was cheating with and went off, making him leave. I was fed up with him trying to have me and the other woman and putting our children on the back burner to play house with her and her child. He also had the father of the woman's child wanting to come after him, which I didn't find out until well after the fact. I also learned that day that he was also snorting pills.

The fight we got into that day was extremely bad, and the police were called by other people that lived in the apartment complex, but I gathered myself together and left before the police arrived. We weren't living together at the time, so when I got back to my apartment, he came over, trying to apologize. I was just so broken and the only thing I could do was cry. The only thing I wanted was for this pain to go away. While he was talking, he pulled out a tiny baggie with tiny blue envelopes with a white substance in it. That is when he told me it was heroin, and that he started doing it not too long before. He then asked me if I wanted to try it because it would help me calm down. Without much thought, I gave in because I didn't want to feel the pain I was feeling anymore; I just wanted to be numb. I snorted my first line of heroin, and it instantly made me stop crying and made me numb. I liked the feeling because I was no longer hurting. I also told myself that it would be the only time that I would ever do it because I didn't want to get hooked. I ended up breaking that promise that I made to myself.

I didn't get hooked instantly. I started doing dope occasionally with my significant other and he was doing it about every day by then. I got increasingly hooked as my tolerance for it went up. There was a time that he didn't have the money to get it and that was the first time I experienced withdrawal. I saw how bad it drove him crazy to be going through withdrawal and I also was feeling horrible without it. The next morning, he found some while we were at his mom's, and he ran out of her house so fast to get it. I never saw him run that fast since I had known him. He got back with it and we both were going crazy trying to get it in our system.

In my mind, I was in denial and didn't think I was hooked. Not just me, but him as well. Love no longer bonded us together. The addiction to the drug now kept us together. I allowed him to move in after a close friend that I shared the apartment with moved out, and I used more.

I eventually started using every day with him and the days we didn't have heroin, we found a quick fix until we got some. We would snort painkillers just to ease the withdrawal.

Our relationship became very toxic. When we would use, both of our tempers were short and if one little thing didn't go right, we would say very hurtful things. He would say, "You wonder why we don't have sex anymore? Because I don't want you," and then I replied, "I don't need you to have sex with me because I'm being taken care of and it's better than you."

He started talking to the other women again, but the heroin made me more confident, so I started talking to other men because I wanted someone who would value my worth when I didn't even know or value my worth. Looking at it now, what I really wanted was love, affection, respect, loyalty, and joy and I was looking in all the wrong places, with all the wrong men, and not in the right ways. I was blinded by lust and an addiction. I also allowed my broken heart to cloud my judgement.

I thought I found happiness in using, but all I did was ignore the pain and problems that bringing me. I could no longer live life or function every day without it. Day by day, I was losing more of myself and the relationship I was in was getting increasingly toxic. I had not felt true happiness since I started using and I no longer felt in love with the man that I had three amazing children with. He was no longer the man that swept me off my feet back in high school. I felt trapped in this relationship but, again, I wouldn't give it up because he was the one who had access to what I needed. Our relationship became abusive–first verbally and gradually, it became physical. After the abuse, we would turn around like nothing happened and get high.

My significant other's mom saw the toll it was taking on us because he was always calling her to ask to borrow money. His mom and grandmother would help us take care of our kids. My family, on the other hand, didn't know anything because I did my best to act as normal as possible around them. If they thought I was under the influence of something, I'd always deny it and push myself further from them because I figured if I didn't really interact with them, they wouldn't be able to ask questions or make assumptions (which weren't really assumptions).

My significant other tried to go to rehab for the first time because it got harder and harder for us to get money to get high and his family told him that either he goes to rehab, or they would no longer help us. The day we dropped him off at rehab, I *thought* I was so emotional because we were always together, but I was actually emotional because I would have to go through full-blown withdrawal by myself and still be a mom at the same time. While he was in rehab, I went through withdrawal for two days and by day three, I felt better and clearer-minded. I felt like I had no desire to go back to heroin and that we would have a fresh start once he got home. He was gone for 21 days, and I was able to stay clean–but only for 21 days.

The day he came home, we picked him up from rehab, got something to eat, his grandmother dropped us off at our apartment and she gave him some money before we got out the car. We went into the apartment, and he told me all about his experience in rehab. Then suddenly he said that a part of him wanted to text his dealer to just see if he would answer him because he wanted to tell him he was home from rehab. The day we dropped him off, I deleted the dealer's number out of my phone, but the number was the last number in my call log, and he knew it was the number once he saw it. I didn't realize that I only deleted the contact, and that it didn't erase the number in the call log, so he got ahold of the dealer. He made small talk with him at first, telling him about rehab and then he asked him if he was good (meaning did he have any dope). At first, the dealer didn't really want to answer, but before I knew it, my significant other was on his way to meet up with the dealer. At first, I was upset because he had just gotten home. We both had 21 days clean, and I told myself I wouldn't go back, but he insisted we would only do it that day, and so I ended up giving in and we got high that day. It took no time at all before we were back to using every day.

We were back to struggling and not having any money, so I applied for jobs and got hired back at the job that I had a couple of years prior, working at a department store. I tried balancing a job, an addiction, being a mother, and taking care of my household. The first week at my job didn't start off the way I wanted it to; I was sexually harassed by a supervisor in another department I had just met the day I started back there. After the first encounter, I spoke to the assistant manager to let him know what happened because I felt disgusting. He had me write a report but nothing else happened afterwards. Nothing happened to him. He kept his job, and he continued to harass me, which was another painful weight added to me, which is why I started using before work. It was the only way I could deal with the sick comments that he would make every day. I was then made aware by other co-workers that I was not the first one that he has done this to. There were a couple of other women that he harassed, but neither of them reported it. They told other co-workers but didn't go to management about it, and I think one woman ended up quitting.

I managed to get through the first year of working at my job doing well with balancing work and using because I needed to not only take care of my children but also take care of my significant other and my addiction. My significant other briefly had a job which gave us extra money to pay bills and to use, but he ended up losing it for being high at work and passing out on the job. His supervisor sent him home the night he passed out, and he had to go in the next morning for a drug test, which he declined to do because he knew he was going to fail it and get fired anyway. So, we were back to only one income–my income.

At this time, we were doing dope three to four times a day and would use most of my paychecks to get high, so we went through my paychecks fast. I would get paid on a Thursday and not have money by Tuesday, and we would have to wait another week until I would get paid again. My significant other had a new dealer he had known since school, and he told him he would trade some of my food stamps for some dope. The dealer agreed, and that became another way for us to feed our habit.

One day before we were about to use, my significant other admitted using heroin another way, which was in a syringe. I told him I would keep doing it the way we had always done it, but each time we would do it, I would get more and more curious about how it felt to shoot it up instead of snorting it. One day, I gave in. After that day, I was beyond hooked and what little morals I had left were completely gone. Every time I looked in the mirror, I no longer recognized the person standing there. The person I saw in the mirror had nothing but darkness around them and they looked defeated and fully controlled my something evil. It scared me to look at myself, but it was not enough to quit because now that I was shooting up, I was in way too deep. I stopped looking at myself in the mirror and this is when I became a true slave to this demon.

I didn't get to make it a full two years into my job because I was fired, but before that, I lost my food stamps for not reporting that month, so my significant other told his dealer that I would take items from work for him in exchange for the heroin. The first few times I said no because I did not want to lose my job, but as our hunger for the dope grew, I agreed to doing it. The first time, I was very scared to get caught, but I made my way out the building with the items without being detected and gave it to my significant other to take it to the dealer in exchange for the heroin. The more we craved dope, the more willing I was to take from my job when the dealer would ask for something specific or if we did not have the money to get high.

One day my luck had run out, and I got caught on the camera taking items that morning. I was called in the office and once I saw security, I confessed to what I did, and I was arrested. I was carried out in handcuffs in front of customers and co-workers. At that moment I was so ashamed and disappointed in myself. That was the first moment I was no longer numb. I was sent home after getting fingerprinted and having my picture taken, and I was told that I would receive my court date in the mail. Not too long after that, I was evicted from my apartment for allowing my significant other to stay there after he was banned from the apartment complex.

One Sunday, a month after I got arrested and lost my apartment, I went to my mom's church for their afternoon service. During the altar call, I had this strong desire to go up to the altar for prayer. My significant other and I were about to get up and leave during altar call, but when I tried to leave, I could feel this force pulling me up to the alter. I tried to walk against it, but I felt it pushing me backwards to the altar. I stopped trying to fight what I was feeling, and I turned around and walked to the altar. As my mom and the guest preacher put their hands on me, this powerful rush came over me; I could feel this disgusting dark force trying to wrap an evil spirit around me and I began to scream, *"GET OFF OF ME, GET OFF OF ME... GET AWAY FROM ME!"* I could feel the power of God ripping the evil force off me and as he did this, I felt my mind getting clearer and God showing me he had me. All he needed for me to do was take a step and trust him. After losing everything I once worked hard for, I tried to make a step and try it God's way because I failed when I walked away from God.

I did not change overnight; I still did heroin, but for a very brief time after that day because after that service, whenever I would shoot up, I felt that guilt and shame that I never really felt before. My significant other was living in another state at this time, and his grandmother offered to let me and my children move in with them. That is how we got our fresh start.

I started going to a clinic for drug and alcohol counseling and for medication to help get me off the heroin. I was going there for three months and my significant other and I were both doing good in our program when he had to go to court for past charges and he ended up getting sent to jail for a month. I started going back to church during this time and was getting closer to the Lord. I had testified for the first time, thanking God for saving my life, because if it was not for him, I may not even be alive to see another day and see the amazing things he wanted to do in my life. I went home feeling ready to start the week.

That Tuesday, I got a call from the state police saying that I missed my court date and that they had mailed me the date. My heart felt like it was breaking because my mail went to my mom's address and she gave me every bit of mail that I received, so it couldn't have been sent to her house. After telling the trooper I would turn myself in once I get a public defender, he sent a fugitive warrant to the state that I moved to. I was picked up that night and sent to jail.

The first night in jail was really a revelation because I had never been to jail before. While I was in there, I prayed, "Lord, I have been doing so well, and Sunday I gave my testimony. How did I end up in this?"

I heard God say, "The devil is mad because you chose me. You also must pay for the mistakes you made. Continue to trust in me and focus on me, and I will bring you through all of this."

From that moment, I trusted him, and he protected me the seven days I was in there. I stayed in his word while in there and he brought me through my case. I could have ended up with a felony conviction, but God made a way. I got four years of probation and with God, I got off in four years when most can't get off in the time they are given. I haven't gone back to heroin, and I am such a victorious woman that overcame something that many struggle so much with and lose their lives to every day. It took me making a step to put faith and trust in God. He rescued me and is still molding me into the strong courageous woman he had destined me to be.

Latricia Pipkin

About Latricia Pipkin

Latricia Pipkin is a high school graduate, mother of three, wife, and recovering addict. She has been sober for five years now and feels beyond blessed to be alive. Latricia has an older sister and brother, and they were raised by their mother, who is truly the definition of God's love. Her mother is truly her best friend. Latricia is very driven, strong-minded, blessed, free, and an independent queen who is ready to continue to level up in every aspect of my life—not just to the levels she wants to reach, but to the levels God has already planned to take her.

"This assignment was designed to help me heal properly."

Selara Gatewood, "Positioned for the Promise" ♦ *V1*

RIPPED, RAISED, RESTORED

Trish Thompson

The Ring Wasn't Worth My Life
I signed up to be his lawfully wedded wife
Not his personal doormat of disrespect
Nor his punching bag using my neck
Whenever he desired,
Or him being infuriated with me
Asking questions he didn't quite like
I was blinded by his charm
White teeth, smooth glide, sweet suits with jokes on the side
My realization just came alive
I've two stepped with the devil straight from the depths of hell
Didn't know it was going to damn near cost me my life
To be in this mental jail
Being caged like a battered bird,
Broken clipped wings, never to fly again
To take this aggressively abusive ride
This flawless diamond I accepted to be his bride
His beloved right hand by his side
Had secrets nobody could see through
Being beaten into submission, suffering in silence too

The Ring Wasn't Worth My Life
The house held me captive day and night
Trapped me as its hostage

No voice of my own
Devoured me as its lunch snack bite after bite
My right hand index finger gripped by his tight teeth, nearly bitten off
With a scar, marked for the rest of my life
To remind me of my husband's deliberate domestic violence beatings
Which he thought were an amusing sight
Blowing his sin sick breath in my face,
As if he was performing voodoo with his colorful calculations of lies
Being chased like an animal through the jungle,
Through the hallways of this house of pure hell
To walk past mirrors that unveiled his inner demons
It was never a home in my sight –
Always left me feeling like a distant stranger so full of fright
Being pissed off was his program
To put me in my proper place
By his domineering gross negligent behavior,
Because he is mad about responsibility & getting caught in infidelity
My showers are monitored with his peeping tom like creeping –
Always reminding me, pointing his finger upwards
"I got my eye on you & my cameras see you too."
Takes tally of trash each and every morning to see what I'm eating
When to get up, when to lay down
What to wear and I better not frown
My restaurant menus and napkins snatched from my trembling lap
As I go to turn my back in embarrassment,
You better not order that dessert or you will get a backhand slap

The Ring Wasn't Worth Me
Not being cherished as the true hidden treasure GOD says I am
The hands that were supposed to hold me
Were the hands that choked me and controlled me
The heart that was supposed to love me was full of hate, venom, and jealousy
The weight of love is supposed to captivate the heart
Not crush, navigate, or manipulate!
The entrance of this invisible gate leads to a devastating doorway

of doom

The Ring Wasn't Worth My Life
This fairytale wasn't written quite right
To have and to hold though I thought was true
No white picket fence for me
Only the vows that always left me black & blue
Becoming married to this monster was the worst thing to do

This Ring Wasn't Worth My Life
In sickness and in health till death do us part
Was a scheme and a plot from the start
To honor and to cherish, I never received
Just a signed contract, signature of my own blood, you see
Becoming Mrs. Michael David Thompson came at a very high cost
Not aware of his shady criminal background
My emotions were taken hostage and let down and lost
I felt amazingly overwhelmed with grief, no love
And my feelings played upon on & off
From his injustice of brutality,
Never knew from one day to the next who I would see
The Demon, My Husband, or The Most Evil Devil he could be
Moved and maneuvered me as if I was a chess piece on his shelf
My peace of mind, my freedom he kept for himself
I just handed delivered my kingdom keys to a thief, a liar, and a cheat
My well of living waters in jeopardy of pollution from a deceiver of unsanctified streets,
Deafen my inner spiritual ear of my heart
Played me for an absolute fool of make believe
How could I ever think this imposter ever really cared anything about me
To be robbed blindly by this devil and left to hemorrhage in this abusive defeat
Though he tried it!
Every way he could rip my reputation!
To tear into my self-esteem and confidence completely
Shattered my heart beyond belief to break me spiritually
"Who's gonna take a chance on you?"

Tell people I am no good!
That I am not called, that I am crazy
That I am not anointed, but I am lazy.
Discredit my character!
Dismantle my ministry!
"You will never preach, pray or speak God's Word, nor shall your spiritual gifts ever advance if given the chance!"

This Ring Wasn't Worth My Life
To become a hostage of pain, fear, shame and strife
Paralyzed by punches that became patterns day and night
Praying upon a shooting star passing by my bedroom window from a far
If only I had wings to take flight
I would fly so far away from here
My tears became my best friend
Way deep down from within
My bible wide open as my pillow for my head
The word of GOD as the balm as I bleed
That held the pieces together as I held on to hope
To mend my broken & busted heart hanging by life line's rope
Totally ripped wide open, severed from end to end
Never realizing saying yes, I will be your forever wife
I would be stabbed in the back with his hidden gaslighting knife

Being swept off my feet was to be lifted up off our garage floor
To be strangled and dangled with his rough rage and roar
The scent of Satan directly in my face
To feel the spit on my flesh, I will never erase
All I saw was death in his eyes from a deep, dark unwanted place
I am of light staring all this adversity straight in my face
This atmosphere is of pure reckless unrighteousness,
Saying to myself, "How did I get in such a low, undeserving space?
What did I do for him to hate me? Why wasn't I good enough?
Why doesn't his love flow
For me like his women of the night?
Why didn't his heart skip a beat for me
Like her messages leaped for him?"
"I miss you… I love you… can't wait to see you."

Why won't he let me and my broken, scattered pieces go?
Since his actions clearly love them & not me! And it shows!
I'm just the misfit toy of Christmas past.
His flirtatious ways lights up their eyes while all I do is sit, weep, and cry

This Ring Wasn't Worth My Life
If only I had not taken that beautiful box
Puffed and pulled satin black bow
I would have understood the very concept of saying no!
The very first time I refused it all,
My Husband, My Love, slammed my head over and over into our kitchen wall
He says, "You don't tell me no, nor do I accept your rejection!"
"Your damaged goods, not a blessing.
I thought I was getting an upgrade with you.
You're just another bad mistake I made. I regret my decision to even marry you."

His damaging & degrading comments
His dysfunctional toxicity
I would hear and feel in my gut
Over and over every day
"I'll take you to the ER to get you checked out. You better not tell 'em it was me that beat you, tossed you and punched you out."
"No damage to the wall, no damage to your head, just go to bed."
"You ain't got no tubes running through you, you don't have no glass eye."
"You ain't dead, you'll be alright, no need to cry!"
Standing in complete disbelief,
Just shaking uncontrollably
With my head held in my pulsating hands.
This man has no sense of remorse or he just don't comprehend
Uncontrollable tears turn to pure fear
Trapped in a nightmare with my eyes wide opened
At this point, I would just rather commit suicide
To make the pain stop instead of having to run and hide
Limping day to day with all this pain all boxed up inside
This is unrealistic, man made puppet mastery in disguise

The Ring Wasn't Worth My Life

Being yanked, snatched, and dragged like a rag doll in the presence of GOD
I took a savage beating on my very own
Ebenezer AME Zion church yard.
While dazed, limping and trying to get to safety
He proceeded to feed my head to our SUV's passenger side door window
While the old timer's Mr. Jimmy, Rev. Lester Champion, Ronnie the bass player just stood there watching me being bullied, beaten in public humiliation
Then trying to get counsel from my church
To be told by Co-pastor Rev. Reo J. King: "You think pastor gonna help you or run to your rescue? That's a personal matter we can't help you."
My church is supposed to be my safe haven although I thought
I have never felt so betrayed, bewildered, lost and distraught
From a church which I was brought up in born and raised to this day

My Ring Wasn't Worth My Life

To watch in sheer, unpleasant, irrevocable disgust
My supposed-to-be-husband, my lover, my friend
My supposed-to-be-protector till the end
Gently, puts his bass guitar over his right shoulder
Walk up the steps into our house of worship
And play for Old Timer's rehearsal without a blink of his own eyes
As if he had not just committed the worst violation to me, my body, my heart, and all of my mind
My soul had just been stripped of all respect for this disrespectful bully in boots
I have been ripped, tattered, and scarred from my emotional roots

This Ring Wasn't Worth This Continued Level of Horror

Now back to the house of drama
Full of nonstop childlike immaturity
I am yelling and screaming for Barbara Mechelle to save me from this aggressively vicious attack upon my very life

This man so full of devious unstableness
"Just do something! Do anything! Just get him off me!"
She just sits there in our kitchen area unmoved and motionlessly
My husband's dead weight crushing and suffocating me
I know that this is the day that surely will be my early demise
My premature death lying lifeless upon our living room floor
My goals, my dreams, my aspirations never to come true
My lifelong mission of becoming a philanthropist to give to others as GOD has given upon to me

This Ring Is Not Worth
My body being crushed, distorted and disfigured beyond anyone to recognize
Gasping for just a single breath, just a single breath for me to survive
The major thought going through my mind:
Is this what I earned? To be a beloved bloody valentine? An abused, unhappy bride?
What happened to my life, my lover, my friend?
The awful image of my jewels of life
Having to identify their dear Mama
Cold slab, body bag, and toe tag
Not even a chance to say any goodbyes

The Ring Wasn't Worth My Life
To be in the company of a deceiver, an imposter, a counterfeit, a chameleon of camouflage
A liar that tells lies to seek attention.
Ego that is weak, that kept me isolated from other women
A bully that boost and brags
Total kryptonite to my matrimony of being married to this man full of madness
Deep-seated unresolved issues
The mystery mad masked man lying awake within his tissues

The Ring Wasn't Worth My Life
Choosing a ring instead of choosing GOD's best
Trusting the image of a man instead of discerning the spirit of this man

If only I tried the hand before I trusted that hand
My husband is a perpetrator hiding in plain sight
Never turn a blind eye to red flags, they are always right
If only I had asked the right questions
When I knelt to pray each & every day
Letting my ways be of the LORD
Leaving all consequences to almighty GOD,
Would have afforded me the luxury of never experiencing this torturous nature
Directly to my bleeding & broken heart

This ring did not promise me protection
Nor did it keep me safe
It wasn't worth being thrown out like Thursday's trash in my own driveway
At the residence of 4 Rapid Run Road, which is now my past
My personal belongings being tossed into Glad hefty bags
I am placed on front street for the entire world to laugh and see
But my husband did me a huge favor, you see
His unacceptable behavior showed me who he really appears to be
To turn, walk past me as he never knew me
Like an echo of a kiss-less whisper in the wind

The Ring Wasn't Worth My Life
To be entangled by an angel in the world
But mangled by a monster behind closed doors
Mask of controlling manipulation
The betrayal, the disrespect, the public humiliation
My husband, the perpetrator, plays the victim quite well
But I was his prey each and every day in a house full of pure hell
Having to hear his lips say over and over repeatedly
"You can't afford to live in my house and you can't afford to leave my house"
Rang out with a thunderous force, loud and clear from the north to the south

This Ring Wasn't Worth
Him stealing my social security card, birth certificate for identity & tax fraud,

Plotting my premature death like a scene from *Lifetime* movie
Secret burial in our backyard, he would be through with me
But for GOD afforded me blessing of escape and snatched me back from the hands of the enemy on April 09, 2020, at 10 am early that Thursday morning
Clearly hearing an inner voice saying to me, *"If you do not leave this house today–not tomorrow, not even in the next hour, nor next week–he is going to kill you."*
The Holy Spirit gave me the wherewithal of His power, strength, and peace to move my feet without hesitation!
GOD saved me from future embarrassing altercations
So now I can live my best life for my LORD and Saviour Jesus Christ!

This Ring Wasn't Worth
My car being taken away
I am forced to walk on any given day
But it's ok. GOD said in his word
Which is spirit and life
That I am not hard pressed or perplexed
All my blessings are pressed down, shaken together and runneth over!
He would restore all back to me one day
If I would just suffer a little while for his name's sake
If I just keep still and my mind stayed on him
The LORD will fight everyone of my battles
Be of good courage and very good cheer
He will strengthen thine heart
"For you are my daughter, for I am LORD GOD, I shall never depart
So nothing that the enemy does shall overshadow my blessings for you
I shall see you right on through
Put your trust in me, not mortal man
I am the lifter, no need to walk upon sinking sand
For I am your fortress and foundation
A rock from which you stand."

Though The Ring Wasn't Worth It
I hear the voice of GOD saying:
The ripping was necessary

To prepare you, not punish you
By cutting you deeply, I can use you greatly
To raise you is to restore you
Being tattered and torn is not your punishment
If I can not trust you in your pain,
I can't trust in your palace
Though tragedy is what you went through

The Ring Wasn't Worth My Life
It was worth going through the hell coming through the other side of the flames
You meet adversity head on, now it knows your 1st name
To trust you with your pain is to allow you to rule and reign
In order to elevate you, I had to separate you from places, people, and things
That were a threat to your higher self & creative being

The Ring Wasn't Worth It
But I am your LORD Thy GOD
I am worth every tear you shed
I am worth every bruise you bore
I am worth every lie you were told
I am worth all of your obedience to hear my voice
Never separate from me because of your bad choice
Choose me this day and forever more
I have the keys to all your freedom going forth

Though The Ring Wasn't Worth It
The strength I gave you to place your hands on the door was worth more
The courage I gave you to walk out that same door was worth waiting for
The wisdom I gave you to never look back, never reopen that door
Now you are free
Whom the Son sets Free is free indeed

Humble is the way
Your blessing was in your breaking
Your pain was not the problem
It was the antidote to your solution
The pain pushed you perpetually to your purpose
Now you're a beautiful butterfly, free to pursue all your passions
To kiss the dew of the morning glories

Lay your hands upon your new found happiness of disconnection,
Welcoming the challenges, for you learned how to dance in your storms and smile while it was raining

I Know The Ring Wasn't Worth Your Life
But I allowed these things
Even Satan to disrupt your peace
Yes, you lost everything
But I didn't allow you to lose your mind
I am your keeper!
I am the lifter of your head!
Stop saying you're failure
When all you did was fall forward successfully
Your desperation positioned you perfectly
It required you to fall on your face
Stop, pause, and pray
You are created in my perfect image
You will always win as I defend!

The Ring Wasn't Worth It
But your survival brought you back to me
Now you're back on track towards your destiny
Your birthright
Your inheritance
This is not your end
This is your beginning
Wipe your slate clean and begin to live for me
But seek 1st of my kingdom, and all my righteousness.
I shall add all things unto you
Bring all unto me
Your heart, mind, body, and spirit

The Ring Wasn't Worth Your Life
But I come to give you life and give it more abundantly
So you see evil may have showed up at your door slick & silver tongued
Proud and boastful
Suited and booted full of demonic operation
Meant you no good, as it may have seemed
I was there the whole time, behind the scenes

You may not have seen me I was surely there
Covering you, your life with great care

The Ring Wasn't Worth My Life
I have angels charge over you no matter where you are
The enemy may come one way but will flee seven
This, you surely have read and know is true
Blessings of escape will always capture & cradle you
A continuous fiery hedge of protection I shall bestow upon you
You are my child. I love you near or far, don't you know?
No matter what the enemy does or says
I got your back girlfriend, you better go on and be great
You are a hearer not just a doer of what my word said

Don't be concerned with blessings that have gone by
I got them stored up in heaven for you way up high
You just keep looking up
Never giving up praying–that's what you do
You cast all your cares upon me
I carry those burdens for you
Those bags of guilt, hurt, and shame
Give them all to me for I am able to bear all your pain

Now after this please learn the lesson of spiritual discernment
Everything that comes knocking at your front door
Is not worthy of you, your peace, love, or your unspeakable joy
You are unique, authentic and beautiful and very loyal
Though your crown may have tilted within this mess
You are still a queen nevertheless
You are clothed in Christ
Adorned with a garment of praise and bought with a price you never have to repay
So learn from this and teach others well
Because there will be other obstacles, this I can tell
But you're stronger now and wiser too
Make the most of this experience and become a better you

The Ring Wasn't Worth Your Life
It didn't feel good, nor did it look good

The most amazing feeling after all is said and done
To forgive Michael David Thompson,
To forgive Patricia Ann Thompson,
To let each spirit go their separate ways
To embrace true love in a healthy way
Focus on the love and not the loss between you two
Holding or harbouring hate, bitterness or any malice like fools
Praying that GOD touches and turns my once beloved heart
That he may also be healed
Set free from the world demonic darkness

The Ring Wasn't Worth My Life
The blessing in the breaking is what I am taking
Brought me back to my first love
The lover of my soul
GOD's embrace and all his sweet, sweet connection of conversations
Taught me how to now set personal and professional boundaries
To use my mouthpiece of communication as a tool of love, not war
Not to stoop to the devil's ditches just because a narcissist has bad intentions
Knowing that I may be broken, I am still beautiful
GOD can and GOD will use each & every one of my scattered & shattered pieces
Which makes me a walking, living, breathing miracle and testimony
I don't have to start over from square one
Just get up from where I am and run
Forgetting those things which are behind me
Pressing towards the things in front of me
Knowing that my life is not over
Now I can turn my pages of chapter two
Getting moving and do as GOD instructs me to
Living for Jesus is what it is all about
Seeking his kingdom first
And letting him figure it all out

Though The Ring Wasn't Worth My Life
The test and trial made it alright, alright
Now I have focus, vision, and clarity

Pursuing my purpose and all that is created inside of me
The pity parties and sobbing are over
Time to tighten up the seat belt and start soaring over and over
Like the eagle that I was created to be
Not walking around with my head held down in agony,
Feeling busted and disgusted
That's not who GOD created me to be
Strong, black, confident, a force to be reckoned with
That's Me!

The Ring Wasn't Worth My Life
But it brought me to the doorway of light
To be encouraged by my HOPE
To be motivated by my LOVE
To be guided by my DREAMS
To focus on the good and perfect gifts from above
Was worth all GOD's favor and unconditional love
All my trust, all my belief, and all my faith was wrapped in his embrace
That he would continue to be the lamp under my feet and the light to my pathway.
To redeem me, release me, and set me free
I am not forgotten, I am not forsaken, but I am forgiven

Living with pure purpose and intelligence That's the life for me
To walk tall
Head held high
Never giving in
Never ever giving up will be my alibi
The devil thought this would be the very end of me
The pain would pursue to crush me
Beat me
Subdue me
My dreams shall never die
The pain is what I needed to get by
I gained more momentum to strive and survive
Though I went through the worst hell imagined
On this side of the sky
My husband says no one will believe me no matter who I tell

The power of my tears and testimony say they will
I am filled with the fire of the Holy Ghost surrounded by Queens
That are full of life, good intentions and talents they bring
Now I have a tribe that stands in agreement with me & right by my side
Future challenges that may arise
I am no longer alone or a casualty of calamity
But a survivor of who I am truly destined to be
A strong, anointed, appointed, appreciated Black queen–that's me!

Trish Thompson

About Trish Thompson

Her smile says it all! Patricia Ann Thompson is an Evangelist of the Word of God and a dedicated full-time caregiver, loving others back to life one heartbeat at a time. She is a fearfully and wonderfully made mother of three jewels of life and grandmother of four moving munchkins. Her motto is "2LiveIs2Travel" and her motorcycle is her stress reliever medication. Her hobbies include skydiving, motorcycling, fishing, writing, DIY crafts, and any adventurous activity that raises her adrenaline. She strives to encourage, educate, inspire, influence, mentor, and motivate millions of people to be encouraged by their hope, remain motivated by their love, and guided by their faith. Her passion is philanthropy, and my purpose is to be blessed to be a blessing to others in this world. She is no longer paralyzed by fear.

"I may waiver, I may struggle, but I keep going!"

Erica M. Allen, "Loss and Lessons" ♦ *V1*

SOMETHING ABOUT THE NIGHT

Annette Star

I sat in my bed, and the memories flashed through my mind.

Even in a flashback, I was looking for consistency, and yet a pattern I could not find.

As my thoughts came, they often felt so real. I looked back and tried to gather them all and understand why I feel the way I feel.

I often wonder if all the things that will take place in the future are all based on the past.

Another confusing thing I have struggled with is which happened first, and which happened last.

It's like a puzzle with over a thousand pieces, and I just can't seem to remember where everything fits.

There are so many scattered parts all over the place and sometimes one just pops up and really hits me.

I can visualize certain moments as if I'm right there right now.

Triggers from a memory can take me places I don't want to go because I made a vow.

Never to tell or say it out loud; I am so afraid people will find out somehow.

I tried to ignore them, meaning the uninvited thoughts, for such a long time; it just never seemed right.

But now I know why it is so scary, and it's something that I don't like about the night.

Who is that? She has something she wants to say to me, but it's so hard for her to get it out.

But why do I feel so small and incapable of speaking up for myself? What is the real reason I zone out?

It just doesn't seem to make sense.

Every time I have an overwhelming feeling and cannot speak, here comes that little girl on the other side of the fence.

She always seems to show up at the right time, except the strange thing about it is that no one else can see her except me.

I feel like I know her, but why would she want to talk to me? I could be in a room full of people and even walk by a mirror and still sometimes not feel seen.

She tells me to come play with her. Nobody will see or hear. For moments at a time, I don't know if I am dreaming or if this is real.

I walk over towards her slowly, and then suddenly there's that voice I don't like to hear.

It seems as soon as I am close to her, she must leave. Dang! Time must be flying because I felt like I just got here.

I felt like, finally, someone was about to read my mind and say out loud what I have always feared to say.

But I can't! We'll all get in trouble if any of us mention it, so typically we all just pray!

Young & immature, not understanding what I am even alive for.

There was a time I just wanted to sleep, but they thought I didn't want to live anymore.

Older & confused, feeling emotionally battered and bruised;

Does anyone even like me? I know they love me, at least that's what they say.

I am not such a bad girl, like Nan would say, or so I think…

Falling into a deep depression, sink, sink, sink

What is the right way to love your children?

How are we supposed to know what love even looks like?

I thought that since I did not feel this at home, maybe one of the guys in the neighborhood could help me, you know? Maybe Keith, or Pauly, or what about Mike?

It was a hot summer day, and I couldn't believe JC was willing to play with us.

We were around eight years old, and her dark skin just seemed to brighten my entire day,

Becoming best friends, walking to school together became our thing. We would often roller skate since we did not have to catch a bus.

I convinced myself for so long to not say it out loud.

But she was my best friend. How could I not tell her?

"Because we're not allowed!"

But finally, I had a friend who made me feel safe, so I told her.

You did what?

Yes, I told her about what had been happening to me.

You mean us?

No, me! She was my best friend and you she can't see!

From playing house with the neighborhood boys to break dancing on the boardwalk,

She was the best part of my childhood!

She never judged me, and she kept my secret.

You mean our secret?

No, *my* secret!

Who the hell am I talking to?

Do you see now why I hate the night?

My best friend didn't know the battles I faced with all these many faces of me

But I loved being in her presence; it was the safest place for me, just having fun and feeling free.

Nan wouldn't let me stay out after dark, though.

She said, "Little girls had no business out when them street lights came on!"

By this time, I was past pretending and past hiding by faking being mean

I was hurt and scared at home when the night hit

I just wanted to be seen.

Do not fret and do not cry, you're a mom now and you haven't told anybody yet. Why?

My time never lasted very long in one place, so I never even knew how to just be okay with who I was or even with looking in mirrors at my own face.

I do not recognize you, and why are you telling me things are going to be okay?

Where were you a few years ago or even just the other day?

Why can't I be good? Am I just a bad seed?

Who else wishes they had brothers and sisters, so for a change, someone else could bleed?

I sometimes feel lonely and like there's no one to talk to.

Asking myself questions like who can I run to?

Oh Lord, who is this one looking at me all crazy, standing in the mirror holding this baby

Hold on, but I'm still pure… or am I?

Why are you so surprised? she asked

Remember, we were all there every time you laid in any bed.

I asked her as I looked in the mirror: *why now?*

You were being rebellious. Now it's time we tell us.

But you all were there with me… why do I have to say it to you?

It's not for us to hear it. This is just for you!

Here comes that voice again.

Is it already night? Shhh or fight.

I do not want to always do the things I do, but it is like chasing a feeling that no one has ever explained. I think my mom believes I need a psychiatrist. If only they knew my pain!

She smiled back at me and said, "Do not feel bad, little girl. It was never your fault what they did."

Here comes *that* family member to tell her it is time to go. It is like the truth can never come all the way out because then someone else might know.

Secrets and lies and holding stuff inside. What are we supposed to do?

All these voices inside of my head; am I eight years old, 16, or 22?

I think it was because of my past that my memories are scattered all over the place.

I know I need help. There is help, and I have been asking for help, but will they then call me a head case?

One state, two states, three different schools in one year.

Would anyone ever believe anything I ever said?

Who in which city would even really hear? Hear me cry or scream, or shout, kick, and fight.

All I know is there are so many of me, and I know they all protect me at night.

So here she comes again, and this time she has more than one baby–three to be exact.

I often don't know who is speaking, and it makes me feel detached.

This time, she shared with me she didn't understand why she had kids. She didn't feel worthy and thought something's got to be wrong with this.

I was wondering the same thing, not understanding what it's like to be a mother and what, if anything, did we both miss?

I feel like I should've known, and I shouldn't have been surprised when I saw three of them.

Then again, was it her who had kids, or was this really just me, who doesn't feel like a mother. How is that even possible, and how is this God I say I serve going to help me overcome this obstacle?

I'm definitely older than the last time we met.

At this point, I'm maybe 24, with three kids, but a husband, I did not get.

She would pop in and out, and most times I had no memory of her age.

It was like a play, and I could always see different scenes displayed, except all on one stage. All these voices, whether it's day or night. I cannot figure out who was who when they all came out to fight.

Who did that to you, and when did that take place?

Counselors, therapists, psychiatrists, all in your space.

The only way to get healing sometimes is to talk to someone who doesn't know you.

One challenge is finding out who is attempting to or who has already been controlling you.

I was once told the moment I tried to gain some control, I was out of control.

Who would have thought over 31 years later I'd be in one of my darkest and deepest holes?

They say some never even survive rock bottom and end up bailing out early.

I know some may have thought I wanted to end my life, but I just wanted to put some things up on a shelf. You know, just deal with them later, but they just kept coming faster than I could move my feet.

Then it seemed after periods of good times, I would always be met with defeat.

Here she comes again, and I am wondering if she comes to make things better or worse.

She looks different, acts different, and I have never seen her with a purse.

Who is she and who are the others? Are they all different people I have met over the years or simply different parts of me and all my fears?

I could not have braced myself for the things yet to come.

My life had so many ups and downs, moving all around.

It was hard to know where I was going or where I had just come from.

There was so much chaos, confusion, violence, and even drugs.

What really baffled me was trying to understand why my oldest looked up to thugs.

What is a thug, and why were they so appealing?

Maybe having them in and out of my own life must have kept me from genuinely healing.

Trauma to trauma and blow to blow.

The kids are always affected, just in case you didn't know.

There came a time when I was a single mother of three beautiful kids.

My prayers began to change, not wanting them to experience the things that I did.

Everything I experienced had an effect on them.

Another one of my prayers was to be a bright light in my babies' lives, even if mine was still sometimes dim.

So, after some years had passed, I realized one thing for sure: even when she would come and help guide me through another year, all along one thing was true–she was me and I was her, and I no longer had all those things from my past to fear.

These are just a few memories of the night.

To be continued…

Sonya "Annette Star" Russell

About Annette Star

Sonya A. Russell, aka "Annette Star," was born in San Bernadino, California on Twenty-Nine Palms Marine Corps Base. She is her favorite person's only child–her beautiful mom, Betty L. Hopson, but also has siblings on my father's side. With a father who was in the Marine Corps and who was the former lead singer of The Hues Corporation, she moved around a lot. She graduated from high school in Cincinnati, Ohio despite attending four different high schools in three different states and has had an extremely adventurous life. Sonya began working at age 12 years old and has a diverse professional background, with over 30 years of experience as a Para-Educator, Social Worker/Case Manager, Administrative Assistant, amongst other things. She is the mother of three adult children and a grandmother of six grandchildren. She loves to write, music, educating others, and loves the Lord.

"I had to stay strong for them while breaking on the inside."

T.C. Woodards, "Dismantling Our Happy Home" ♦ *V1*

FAILING IN ORDER TO SURVIVE

Nawanda Turner

"Not everything that is faced can be changed, but nothing can be changed until it is faced." ♦ **James Baldwin**

While I wish I could say my story was a fairy tale, I can't. There was no Prince Charming waiting to rescue me. There were no magic beans that would grow and lead me to a castle in the sky. As much as I love glitter, there was also no fairy dust to sprinkle on all the dysfunction that had transpired throughout this journey. Now, don't get me wrong; my life is not some tragic anthology leaving one to wonder what led to the chaotic events of my life. In fact, it is an ever-evolving journey, one that is filled with highs, lows, twists, and turns, but most of all, self-discovery and growth. So how did the journey even start? It wasn't something that occurred overnight. In fact, there was a series of events that led to me making some serious decisions about the state of my life.

In the summer of 2016, my life turned upside down. I found myself in a situation I could never have imagined for myself and my children.

If you told me I would be facing what I faced in 2016, I would have called you crazy. Why? Because I believed in marriage and the vows I took. When I said, "I do," I believed this would be my person for the rest of my life. However, it was more than apparent by the spring of 2016 I had to make a different choice as it was a matter of life and death.

My son, who I affectionally call "the kid," was preparing to graduate high school and our families were coming into town. This was a happy occasion indeed, as "the kid" was graduating high school and did so while being a double Varsity letter athlete. Knowing my family would be there to celebrate gave me strength because they were truly supportive. The other side of that was full of anxiety because I didn't know how my husband would act around my family. At that point, we were no longer sleeping in the same room, and we barely talked to each other. When we communicated with each other, it was full of elevated decibels and hurtful phrases. There was no positive communication occurring in our marriage and honestly, the sight of him made my head hurt.

Until this point, I had done a stellar job of hiding the extent of the abuse, mistreatment, and disrespect. My family had no idea the depth of what me and my children had endured with him, and I knew it would devastate them. I also didn't know how they would react to the knowledge that I kept me and my children in a toxic and abusive relationship, so I kept this part of my life hidden. Honestly, at this stage, I was in straight survival mode.

Despair, hopelessness, and defeat are words I would use to

describe my situation. My life felt like it was spinning out of control, and I had no way of escape. I didn't know the start from the end, and I felt like I was in a non-ending maze of chaos. Few people knew the pain I was in as I continuously put on my mask, which always included a smile; a smile which prevented people who didn't know me well enough from asking, "What's wrong?"; a smile that masked the hurt, the pain, and the utter disappointment I continuously endured; a smile that allowed me to continue a charade that drained me every day; a smile perfectly placed to ward off any suspicion of what was really going on in my life. I kept up this charade until my life came to a place where I couldn't take it anymore. It was literally taking the life out of me and something had to change.

"*You may not control all the events that happen to you, but you can decide not to be reduced by them*" ♦ Maya Angelou

The events leading to the summer of 2016 caused me to make a choice for me and my children that challenged my understanding of what it meant to fail. Merriam Webster defines failure as *"a lack of success in some effort or a situation of occurrence in which something does not work as it should."* I didn't want to be a failure in my marriage. For years I had seen the red flags in my marriage, walking on eggshells and my heart racing every time the garage door opened, not knowing if he had consumed alcohol before coming home and to what degree of aggression I would be facing. The angry outbursts and inconsolable rage, the excessive drinking and illicit gambling, the frequent disappearances and missing items from the house combined with the refusal to take part in mental health or couples counseling were all telltale signs that I should have run for the door and never look However, I didn't because I felt like that was not an option av to me. I was challenged by a belief system that conditioned me thinking a prerequisite for being a strong woman was not having failed marriage. Growing up in the church, divorce was not something talked about unless it was to reinforce the ideology that God hates divorce, and it was a sin. There was also no conversation or resources surrounding how to remove yourself safely from an abusive and toxic marriage. I grew up with loving, committed parents, so I didn't have a blueprint on how to deal with toxicity. However, I had enough. After he denied my many requests for him to seek counseling, I decided I would no longer stay in this toxic situation called my marriage. I told him either he needed to leave, or I would leave. Even though we both were on the mortgage to the townhome, I was willing to walk away and had already started looking for alternative housing for me and the kids. My decision didn't come without its unique set of challenges for me. In my mind, sticking and staying showed the depth of my strength. If I couldn't handle the situation, I felt that meant I was a failure. How could I even process and overcome that mindset, especially since I was never taught what to do when the situation was mentally and emotionally detrimental? I just didn't want to be a failure.

While the thought of failure was paralyzing, the thought of staying in a situation that was literally sucking the life out of me far outweighed my fear of failure. I was suffocating and couldn't breathe. There was no light at the end of the tunnel because my tunnel felt like a never-ending hole to nowhere. I decided it was time for me to fail. *I chose to fail in order to survive.* Little did I know in my failing, I was going to discover a strength and tenacity so intense it would activate something in me that would propel me on this journey of re-discovery. The critical decision to walk away from my marriage has intricately shaped my life since 2016. It was the catalyst to so many events which spearheaded my journey of self-discovery.

When I looked in the mirror, I didn't recognize the person looking back. I had not only lost myself–I didn't even know how to begin the search. When you systematically lose a part of yourself for 22 years, trying to locate yourself can be exhausting. I had to find something that would keep me focused and provide the inspiration needed to dive headfirst into this new chapter in my life. What I didn't know was God had already provided me with that inspiration in the form of the two children I affectionately call Championz.

I knew come hell or high water, I had to survive. I knew the journey would not be easy, but it was necessary. The survival of me and my Championz was now solely my responsibility. It was up to me with God's help. Although I found myself in unfamiliar territory, as I had been married since the age of 24, for the first time I could breathe. I never knew how much stress I was under until I could finally breathe. *But now what?* How was I going to navigate this new chapter in my life? The first thing I did was pray and ask God to help me along this new journey so that it would cause as little damage as possible to an already fragile situation. I needed to show not only my Championz but also myself that this would not defeat me. With both Championz in college, I knew I needed to make some moves career-wise to better provide financially. I previously told God if I was strong enough to walk away, I needed to take care of our needs. If nothing else stays with you from my story, please tuck this nugget in your pocket. *God hears and listens to what you say.* He not only heard me but placed opportunity after opportunity in my path that allowed me to comfortably provide for me and the Championz.

"Failure is an option. Quitting is Not." ♦ Me

By allowing myself to fail I reset the makeup of my mind. I realized that failure was an option, and it didn't define me or make me less worthy. The mind is a powerful tool, and most battles are won or lost before any actions occur based on a mindset. The enemy will use your battles, dysfunction, and pain to keep you in a defeated mindset. Defeated mindsets rarely make any positive forward progress. By failing, I found a place within myself that wanted to move forward. The pain of my failure put me in a position to tap into the greatness that was dormant. Processing and acknowledging the pain helped free me. It wasn't the pain that defined me, it was how I dealt with the pain that was a catalyst for the current path of our lives. I wanted to get better not only for me but for my Championz. They learn by what I show them. I had to show them better. There were times I didn't want to get out of bed because I felt so defeated, but I mustered up the strength to show up for myself daily. I had to show them they were not a product of their circumstances but a product of their decisions. I had to show them that winning is not always about who finishes first, but who learns the most during the journey. I had to show them that even in the eye of the storm, there is a peace that can be found when you put your faith in God.

While some day I will write more about the pain, the focus for this is about the process of self-discovery and healing. This is about what I did after I realized something had to give. This is about what happened once I submitted to the fact it was only God's grace that would enable me to conquer all the obstacles I was facing.

While my journey is still a work in progress, I know sharing my truth is pivotal to my forward progress. I still have bumps along this journey, but I am confident I will continue to find my way. Know there is hope after pain and failure *is* an option. Know that your pain serves a purpose. Don't be ashamed of the pain, as that will keep you from moving forward. It will keep you in a place of defeat, trying to cover up your true self with masks. Acknowledge and process the pain. Get professional help if needed because everyone's journey through pain is different. Don't hide it. Find a support system that will offer you encouragement but not let you stay in the pain. Know you are created to make a difference.

Don't be afraid to fail, because there is life after failure as long as you don't quit.

Nawanda Turner

About Nawanda Turner

Nawanda Turner is a health care IT consultant and entrepreneur. She is an inspiring woman who believes that actions speak for themselves. While she may not say much, she's always looking at ways to improve herself by her actions from the inside out. It wasn't an easy task as a survival of domestic violence, but when she found her voice, she found her strength. She prays her transparency allows someone else to have the strength to fight for their victory. She is a mother of two phenomenal children, who are both entrepreneurs. She is also YaYa to an amazing granddaughter.

"I was apprehensive, but there was a great nudging in my spirit"

AMK Purnell, "A Poem from My Heart, From a Season in My Life" ♦ *V1*

AFTER THE LOVE IS GONE

Pia R. Sheard

"Dear God, when I grow up, I wanna be in love and marry a handsome prince, and he will pick me up on his horse and we will ride off into the sunset together forever. Oh yeah, and Amen, God."

Growing up, I remember saying that prayer on more than a few occasions. It's what I wanted. It was the only thing I thought made me a woman of the future. I wasn't lonely, I wasn't lacking self-esteem. I was a child. I had no clue that what I saw in the fairytales was only a small fraction of the story.

Ok, so at 18, still very naïve, I thought that all that I prayed for way back then as a little girl had come true. Could it be that easy? I met the man of my dreams, or so I thought he was. He was cute, and I was sheltered. We were born on the same day in the same year. I had no clue what it was to have a boyfriend. He didn't either. But here we were.

We were so very different from the very beginning of our relationship. My mother raised her children to be independent. And he was raised seemingly needing his mother for everything. I remember his own family would make jokes about him still being attached to his mother's umbilical cord. For the longest time, although I introduced him to my family, I told them he was just my friend, but his mother and sister came to my job to meet me. It was so weird; I worked at a fast-food restaurant at the time, and he must have told them about me. I guess he didn't move fast enough in introducing me to them because one day while I was at work, this woman and a young girl came to the restaurant, and they stood in front of my register for a long time, just staring at me. I took a couple of orders and filled those orders, and they just stood there. The young girl had one of the biggest smiles on her face, but the woman had a very stoic look about her. She didn't crack a smile at all. Without ever seeing a picture of either of them, I just knew who they were. Eventually, I think I said, "Can I help you?" and when they got close enough, I asked if they were his sister and mother. Or maybe the young girl said she was his sister. I can't remember. But I do remember them just looking at me, and the look of displeasure on his mother's face.

Very early in our relationship, we had our first of many arguments. I will never ever forget it. We were walking through Green Acres Mall. I saw a shirt that I thought would look nice on him, so I told him he should buy the shirt. At first, he said he would not buy the shirt, and I told him I would buy the shirt for him. Of course, he said no, he would get it, but he needed to ask his mother first. I asked why he needed to ask his mother if he could buy the shirt, and he said because I just do. Well, I didn't understand. Here I was, my mother telling me to work for what you want, but if you buy it, make sure you can pay for it. So, I figured he should be able to do the same thing. Well after he called his mother, and she told him it was ok to buy the shirt, I asked why his mother would have to ok the purchase. I swear my question was innocent. But he said why wouldn't I ask her? You don't have to ask your mother when you buy things and I said no. Well, it blew up into a huge argument in the middle of the mall where he finally yelled that it was her card so why wouldn't he ask her to use it.

"Her card!? Why would you have your mother's card? Why don't you have your own?" He said because his mother takes care of him, unlike my mother. It went on and on. By the next time I saw him, he had his mother and family believing that I was jealous of her. To this day, I can't understand why I would have been jealous of someone who was old enough to be my mother. But his family ate it up; they felt I was jealous of the woman. At times, it made being with him difficult because any time I questioned why he did certain things, his family would look at me like I was acting out of jealousy.

Another point of contention was his sister. I always felt that she would do things just because she knew her brother would never stand up for himself or for me. Shortly after we got married, we lived with his parents. On my days off, they would decide for me that I would watch his sister's children. Now, watching the children was never the problem for me. It was the fact that they never gave me enough respect to ask me if it was ok. I brought it up to my husband. When he spoke to his sister about it, she said that's why he married me. So, when he brought it back to me, it was said that it's their culture and just do it because that's what I signed up for. So, from that point on, I felt like I needed to verbalize that I had plans just so that I wouldn't wake up on my vacation and there be children there.

When I first started dating my ex-husband, his friends thought he shouldn't be tied down to just one woman. So, of course, being the follower that I found him to be, he complied with their wishes. He started dating multiple women at the same time. All of them knew about me, but I had no clue about them. One night during one of his games, I went to the bathroom and about four girls followed me there. They walked up behind me and started talking about number 34 being her man and all sorts of stupid stuff. When I washed my hands and turned to leave the bathroom, they all looked me up and down and they laughed. I could have been hurt that night in that bathroom because of his shenanigans, and he wouldn't have even had a clue.

Two weeks before I got married, my sister asked me, "Pia, why are you marrying him?" I think I asked her why she would ask me that and I loved him and blah blah blah. I look back on that time and I realize that was yet another missed opportunity to get out of it.

Our wedding was an amazing event if I do say so myself. Everyone said that they had a great time. I remember walking down the aisle and he told me I looked beautiful. The way he looked at me, you would think that he was totally into only me (I did look beautiful, though). But even there at the wedding, he had to follow protocol and do what he was told to do. The kiss was because his uncle told him to kiss me.

It wasn't what either of us had planned to do. He looked happy, and he did all the things that a new groom should do. At the reception, he hung out mostly with his friends. But when he danced with his mother, the two of them cried as if they would never see each other again. I mean, they were crying hysterically on the dance floor, holding on to each other for dear life. She kept telling him she didn't want him to leave her and that she was going to miss him *so* much. I kept thinking, *Good Lord, lady, we're coming to live in your house for the time being*, and that he didn't shed one tear when I walked down the aisle, but he was crying like a newborn while dancing with his mother. It was disgusting, but a little comical.

Just before I married my ex, I kept having this suffocating feeling every time I thought about marrying him. I mean, I guess I had to love him at some point, and I was attracted to him, but I didn't respect him at all. And I just had this feeling that things weren't right. I just didn't know how to get out of the fast-moving train, but I also knew that I wanted to have his kids one day. I remember talking to my mother one day about the wedding and she said, "Pia, this marriage is going to be a fiasco!" Of course, I got upset and asked why she would say something like that. Because she saw how I reacted to what she said, my mother said, "Oh wait what does fiasco mean again? I meant it's going to be fantastic". My mother knew exactly what she was trying to say. I came to realize that lots of my loved ones had reservations about this man I was about to marry. One of my closest friends saw him in a night club with another woman shortly after he proposed to me. One of my brothers tried to tell me he was seeing other women when he would come to me and say that he saw my ex out with another woman. Of course, when I asked him about it, he would say he was out to lunch with one of his co-workers. Before we got married, I asked my then fiancé where we were going to live. He told me he wanted to focus on one thing at a time. *Let's focus on the wedding and then we'd worry about where we were going to live.* At the time, he was living with his parents. I just wanted to get a house that we could return from our honeymoon and go to. But of course that didn't happen. We got married, and after the wedding, we didn't consummate the marriage on our wedding night like every other couple in the world. We went back to his aunt's house to have an after party because they told him that's what they wanted him to do. I fell asleep on the floor of the living room. And we got up early the next morning and left to go to Aruba.

Aruba was nice, but I still didn't feel like I was on a honeymoon with my new husband. He was good just being in Aruba. First of all, he didn't even want to go to Aruba for our honeymoon. I kept asking and asking. He said no, he didn't like to fly, and he wasn't getting on a plane. His mother told him he needed to go to Aruba and that's why we went on our honeymoon. He didn't want to do anything while we were there, either. I remember there was a glass-bottom boat sunset cruise. I really wanted to go. But he said it was too much money, and we weren't going. So, I sucked it up, and we didn't go.

The day that we returned from our honeymoon, he informed me that he was going out. I told him that was not acceptable, and we argued a little. He said he promised his friends that they could take him out to celebrate his marriage when he came home from the honeymoon. Lies, I tell you. He came home from our honeymoon, went out with his girlfriend, and stayed out all night with her.

So, after maybe a week of being back from the honeymoon, we finally looked for an apartment together. We found the perfect little apartment; two bedrooms, a nice big living room, a nice-sized eat-in kitchen, and even a little dining area. We secured the apartment, but then he didn't want to move in right away. I just didn't understand anything. I asked why he didn't want to move in, and he told me I was always trying to rush everything. I actually moved in without him and stayed there one night by myself. I told him I wasn't coming back to sleep at his mother's house and then he decided it was time for him to act like my husband. After we moved into our apartment, he found out that his girlfriend's cousin lived across the hall from us. Of all the places in all the world, we moved in where his girlfriend spent most of her time. We stayed in that apartment for exactly one year. His excuse for needing to move from the apartment was that he wanted to get a house and we needed to save money. So, we moved in with his parents.

Living with his parents was a headache all its own. His mother would complain to him about me living there with them. She would tell him I was nasty, and that I didn't cook and clean, all sorts of things that were absolutely not true. I would get home at about three or four in the afternoon. I would cook if there was nothing already cooked. I would wash dishes if there were dishes in the sink. While I was there, I made sure that I didn't make too much of a mess or that I stayed out of the way as much as possible, but his mother still complained about my presence. Of course, he didn't do anything to defend me. I never wanted to live with his parents or anyone else, but he felt the need to live there with them so we could "save money." Remember, the only reason that we were there, I found out later, was because the woman that he had an active relationship with (he was having an affair) lived across the hall from us in our apartment. He was trying to escape before the truth was revealed to me.

Seven months after we moved in with his parents, he told me he had been having an affair. He was moping around for about two weeks and every time I asked him what was wrong, he told me nothing. Well, one Sunday, he got up early and said he wanted to go to church with me. He never went to church with me. We went to church, and he looked out of place and uncomfortable the entire time. Later that evening, he asked me to ride with him to take his father to work. I said ok - I didn't usually ride with him, but I was ok going this night.

On the way back from dropping his father off, he blurted out, "I've been having an affair and she said she has genital warts and if you didn't get checked out and you have it, it could cause cervical cancer." He seemed so relieved when he said all of that, but for me, I was so bothered because I was innocent when we met and now, I had to deal with sexually transmitted diseases? I was livid. But I didn't say anything to him the entire ride back to the house. Actually, I just didn't say anything at all. I went to work the next morning like normal. During that day, I made an appointment to be tested for all sexual diseases that my doctor would give me. When I got the results, I was expecting to get some bad, shocking news. Nope, I was completely clean. No sexually transmitted diseases. Thank God. But afterwards, the more I thought about it the more I realized that she only told him that so that I would know about her existence. She wanted him to have to tell me about her. The saddest part about all of it is that what I remember most is not being broken-hearted over the fact that he was having an affair. I remember feeling a sense of relief when he told me. I felt like I had an opportunity to get out of a marriage that just didn't feel like a marriage at all, but I let that opportunity pass me by. I never trusted him after that, and he never did anything to earn my trust. He continued to live his life in the same manner. He continued to see the same woman that almost caused his marriage to fail.

Because of my ex-husband's infidelity, I got a few silent infections that caused some damage to my fallopian tubes. Basically, what that means is that because he enjoyed screwing around, I lost my ability to naturally conceive and maintain a pregnancy. I remember going to the doctor to get the results as to why I couldn't get pregnant or why I couldn't stay pregnant.

The doctor said, "Ms. Easton, getting pregnant is not the problem. It's staying pregnant. When he went on to further explain, he said that I would get pregnant but because one fallopian tube had a toxic poison in it and the other was badly damaged, when the egg makes it through the tube it is already poisoned, and my body just rejects the embryos before they have time to grow. When I asked how that happened, the doctor said it was caused by a sexually transmitted infection.

I didn't get it, so I said, "But how could I get a sexually transmitted infection… I've only been with my husband." My ex turned to me with a slight smirk and asked me, "Yeah Pia, how did you get a sexually transmitted infection?" and then he turned away.

The doctor looked at me incredulously and said, "Mrs. Easton, it's a *sexually* transmitted infection!" I guess that doctor was thinking, *Boy, what a dummy.* But I really just didn't think that anyone could be that hurtful and uncaring about the health of someone that they claimed to love. Thank God, he didn't damage me completely. I was able to have my beautiful babies, but it took a lot to get them here.

When I was pregnant with my girls, I wanted to be just like the women you see on TV. The father of my babies would come home and rub my belly and rub my feet. He would be so overjoyed that he would dote on me. He would talk to the babies in the womb and get me pickles if I asked for them. But I didn't get any of that. Oh, don't get me wrong, he was happy and very excited to become a father. He just didn't show any type of attachment to the belly. I remember a few times I would ask him to rub my back for me and he would do it, but with an attitude. Then came time for my baby shower. His sister threw the shower for me, but when people would tell her how nice everything was she would say, "I did this for my brother… This is all for my brother." Throughout that night, I wondered to myself *If this is for your brother, then why did I come here?* But he saw nothing wrong with any of that.

Before my daughters were born, I remember our friends (the only friends that we had in common) were talking about going to a Jill Scott concert. They asked us to go with them. I asked him over and over again to go to the concert. Finally, he said "I don't like Jill Scott, and

I'm not going to her concert. If you want to go, then go with them, but I'm not going." Everything was always about what he wanted and what he was or would not do. Nothing was ever really about me. He had his friends, and I had mine. He would go out all the time with his friends, but I was never invited to hang out with them. He never wanted me around, and he never wanted to do anything special with me.

When I first left New York permanently and took my daughters to move into the house that he and I were paying the mortgage on and not living in, he was none too happy. He said that I just took the girls away without talking to anyone and his mother really missed the kids. So, it had nothing to do with me leaving. I lived alone with my daughters for two and a half years, but he would come home on weekends. I remember within that time, I would beg him to come home to find a job in the state of Delaware. I would call and talk to his mother and ask her to talk to him and make him come to Delaware to be with his family. I remember her telling me that I was spoiled and that I didn't understand how corporate America worked and that he could just leave his job. She told me again that I was spoiled, said a few other nice-nasty words to me, and I never brought it up to her again. We would argue almost every time we spoke about him moving here and helping me to raise his children. He would make the joke that I was a single married woman, and he would laugh every time he said it. I just felt so very unloved. But the more time went on, the more I realized I didn't even want him around anymore, and not only that, I wasn't in love or in like with him anymore. Honestly, right from the beginning, I couldn't stand him. Actually, if I have to be totally honest, I'm not sure that I ever loved him like a wife should. I couldn't trust him, and I never respected his weakness. I remember one time we went to Georgia when we were first married to celebrate his grandmother's birthday. I felt like such an outsider as I always did when I was around his family. The day that we arrived there, we were at his uncle's house, and we were sitting in his uncle's living room with his uncle, his uncle's wife, two of his cousins (brother and sister), my ex, and me. We were talking and laughing, and I started teasing his female cousin. We were all still laughing. Well, the brother must have gotten upset over something because the next thing I know, he grabbed a cup of water and threw it in my face. My ex looked at me and said, as water ran down my hair and face, "Pia, what are you doing now?" I was so hurt and disgusted by his actions and his lack of respect for me. I just got up and walked away. What's even worse, he didn't even come and check on me. When I finally saw him again, he said to me, "You needed to take some time to cool off." I couldn't believe it.

I remember a time that I spoke up and vented to one of his aunts about how I couldn't stand him and how rude and disrespectful his family was to me, how I wasn't in love with him anymore and I spoke about some things that were said and/or done to me. Well, the one that I spoke to took what I said and went to tell all the others what I said, not that it was a problem because I said it and I meant it. So, he invited me to an aunt's house for a gathering and when I went there, this aunt chastised me and told me I needed to watch my mouth, stop talking about her family and blah blah blah. I just kept looking at him and he said absolutely nothing. This aunt told me I needed to be careful about what I say. Do you think that coward said a peep? Not one single syllable of a word came out of his mouth, but I was used to it, and I didn't really care how they felt about me anymore.

After my daughters were born and he finally came to live with us full time, I knew things were tense, but I still tried to see if we could finally become that couple that just needed each other and no one else. I remember asking him why he married me and he said, "You waited long enough and my family was expecting us to get married." Wow, did that hurt. I bought a book about love languages, and he told me the book was a waste of money and it was stupid. I asked him to go to counseling, and he told me he didn't need counseling, so he wasn't going. I think it was the end for me when I asked him if he loved me or asked him to go on dates or family vacations. He responded the same for both: "I'm in a new phase of life, I just want to be a father." *Just want to be a father? But what the heck about me? I was here before they were. What the heck about me.* At that point, I was done.

I had become so empty with constantly crying and calling people to complain. I knew I couldn't continue to live in the misery that had become my life. The constant disrespect, the lack of affection, and the feeling like we were just existing and not living as a married couple should have pushed me over the edge. So, I prayed. I prayed a lot. I never in my wildest days ever wanted to hurt him or anyone else. However, I felt like he just didn't care about me at all, and it was time for me to care about myself. I had been begging him to love me and be a part of this marriage. However, when everything finally blew up between us, suddenly he became the victim. I became this evil person, and he felt everyone had to know about it. There were several times when I said maybe I should just ask him to move back in. My girls would be happy, and he would be happy. But the more I thought about it, the more I realized that we just didn't fit, and we never did.

Honestly, I was frightened about not being with him and being a single mom. I didn't know how I would make it. My ex-husband had cut off my phone, and he left me with no money. I remember saying to him I needed my phone because that was my lifeline to the kids. I remember pulling into a gas station and trying to get gas, realizing that he had taken all the money out of the joint account. I called him and said I needed money for gas because I needed to go pick up the kids. He told me I didn't deserve anything. When I asked how I was supposed to get to the kids, he screamed through the phone, "Stop using those kids!" then he hung up on me. Thank God I had a credit card. But that was the absolute end for me. I didn't know how I was going to make it, but I just knew that God was waiting for me to get out of the way so that He could make a way for me.

So, I went back to work as a substitute teacher at first, and then I found a full time position, although I worked about an hour away from home. I did a lot of saving at that time. I cut off his phone and got my own. The words that my mother would always tell me started to ring in my head and it began to make sense. She would always tell me no matter what situation you get into, make sure you can always handle it by yourself if need be. So, I refinanced the house to remove him from the deed, then I refinanced again to get rid of that HELOC that he could never explain to me. I didn't know what God's plan was for me, but I knew He wasn't going to leave me in that darkness for long and He never left me alone while I was in it.

I write all of this not to gain sympathy, but to finally heal the wound underneath the scab. I have gone through a lot, and honestly, I believe it was at my own hands. The Holy Spirit was speaking to me during my entire relationship. I knew things weren't right. It is with the grace of God that I could remove myself from the situation and pick myself up no matter how many boulders were thrown at me. So many times, I wanted to just give up and say to him "you win," or that I can't make it without his help. But as much as I wanted to say those things to him, I knew it wasn't true, and that I was determined to succeed. If not for me, then for my daughters, who would look to me to show them that even when we deal with adversity, with God on our side, we can always get back up, dust ourselves off, and move on. I don't miss him or desire to be in a relationship with him again. I don't harbor ill feelings or wish him bad. I just realize that my peace is more important to me than anything or anyone.

Again, I didn't share this little tidbit of my life to gain sympathy, because I am fine and I'm doing well. I share this hoping it will be a source of hope for someone else who may be going through a similar thing. I walked away from that toxic relationship better than I was while in it. And yes, I realize it was all just a very toxic part of my life. He may not have physically beaten me, but he left bruises just the same. I just want to offer encouragement to anyone and let them know that they will be alright. The guilt of leaving will eventually fade away. For me I realize, as I stated earlier, that I never had low self-esteem. However, I may have suffered from a low self-worth. For whatever reason, I may not have felt worthy of being loved the way that I thought I should. I didn't feel like I deserved the happiness that I wanted. So, I accepted the mediocrity that was given to me. I'm just so grateful that God brought me through that trial in my life so that I may be a source of hope for someone else.

Pia R. Sheard

About Pia R. Sheard (Easton)

Pia is a mother, educator, certified life coach, and now an author. She was born and raised in New York. Pia is a natural nurturer and has a passion for helping build self-esteem in others. She loves quiet spaces, but her most special time spent is any time that is spent with her daughters. She has had many trials, but through it all, she realizes those trials were created just for her so that she can use them to help others going through similar situations. Pia loves life and loves to make everyone around her feel welcome.

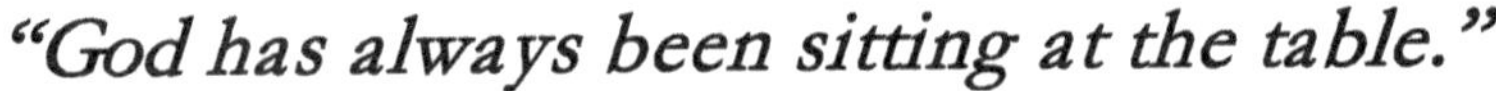
"God has always been sitting at the table."

Tammy Moody, "Tabitha, the Barren One" ♦ *V1*

TRANSFORMATION IN THE EYES OF THE PEOPLE

Tammy Moody

I think about the day God called me to minister the gospel. I was like, "Who, me?"

He said, "Yes, you."

I said, "But I am not worthy, and I am still in my sin."

He said, "Daughter, no one is that good, but *I am.* I am the one that can make you whole. Turn your life around, and I will make you whiter than snow."

I said, "Come on God, I don't want to be no saint, judging other people's lives and telling them they won't make it to heaven because of what they do or don't do. God, that is just too much of a burden to bear."

He said to me, "Just like the burden I bared for you on Calvary, where they stretched me wide, pierced me in my side, and laid the thorns on my head? I still chose to die for you. I knew you before you were even conceived in your mother's womb. I knew what your life journey would entail–some good and some not so good. Yet, as I told the devil, have you considered my servant Job?"

I said, "God, you know I am nothing like Job. I am more like Peter. I have stood for and with you, but when my emotions get the best of me or I want what I want when I want it, I have denied you. I indulged in what felt good or seemed to make me happy."

♦

"Hey Sista girl! You remember when you were singing in the choir with your family at the Church of God and Christ. It was a family affair. Whoop! We sang, "*If anybody asks you where I'm going, tell them I'm going to be with my Lord. I'm going up to yonder to be with my Lord.*"

Another favorite hymn we sang during church service was, "*Be, Be Grateful, Be, Be Grateful. God has not promised me sunshine and that's not the way it's going to be.*"

So, hey Sista girl, we were cruising and moving to the beat of the drums, organ, and piano. Oh, what a glorious time it was, when the Holy Spirit hit just right. People were falling all over the place, as I can remember. As a child, it spooked me at first, but I learned in Sunday school that this happens when we allow God to fill us up and we are truly one with him. We become so thankful for his presence. Well, that is what I got out of it.

*So **Sista girl,** although these were happy times and some not so good times, we grew up thinking that you missed something, like cruising and moving to the beat of the drum.* We should live back in the world, as the grass is greener on the other side. Well, you live a life praising God on Sunday and sometimes during the week. You know what I mean. God still would listen whenever I called him. He is such a loving, unchanging Father.

I believe I was about 10 years of age when my life began spiraling. I still relied on God, and he was my helper in a time of need. As one transitions from a child to a preteen to a teenager and then into a young adult, there is often a "coming to Jesus moment." Jesus is not looking for perfection, but for a willing spirit.

My spirit was always willing. Life created some challenges that my flesh had a desire to fulfill after years of hurt, betrayal, molestation, and addiction, the almost near-death experiences jumping from moving vehicles as an untimely method to take my life because I believed I was not worthy, the promiscuity, which was a means to an end until I found myself again–God's love was still apparent in those times.

In 1989, I surrendered my life to the program of Narcotics Anonymous. The journey of this 12-step process brought me back to a place of developing a relationship with Christ that was more personal. Not my mother's God or my pastor's God. It was personal. As personal as it was, my flesh continued to take over because I felt unloved. I was always searching for Daddy's love. You see, he died when I was two years old, and for whatever reason, there was always a void left in me. I know my mother loved me, and she raised us the best she could. She provided by working day and night to make sure we had what we needed. We grew up in the church. However, I still longed for my daddy and found myself in and out of various relationships.

Sista girl, *I know you can relate!* Searching for love in all the wrong places and settling for sex. The hurt and betrayal continued to rear its head in relationships with the opposite sex.

In 1992, I encountered this feeling unbeknownst to me with my best friend at the time. It was strange, but fulfilling. She understood me. She helped pull me into a place of believing in myself, providing a place of safety with the feelings and emotions I never thought I would ever share. Then one day out of the blue, she kissed me. I was like "What? Umm, no!" That is what my mouth said, but my body and heart were saying *this feels good and she really loves me. I don't have to pretend to like male encounters anymore.*

No*w* ***Sista girl,*** *you know better! You are going straight to hell.* I was confused. So, I denied those feelings as well. I stopped talking to her for a moment, but I couldn't stop thinking about her and how I felt.

It became apparent that we were drawn to each other. I asked God why I was feeling this way. I never waited for the answer. I continued the relationship with T.H. off and on for years, but God never left me as I drifted away from him. He often says he is no respecter of a person. So, I stopped thinking about what others thought about my choices but wondered why they were concerned about my recovery walk and my finances. Excuse me! Were they going to pay my bills? Oh, I think not. I provided for myself, one way or another. Nevertheless, I continued to have conflict between my spirit and my flesh daily.

Sista girl… *How can you love two masters?* I was caught in the grip of a love that I never knew before. It was almost as if it was another addiction. When something so good becomes so controlling, it makes you doubt everything. I was in a seven-year cycle of "on again-off again" relationship with T.H. and became intrigued with other associates that developed into relationships that had become years of her, him, them, or just her.

While enrolled in graduate school, I met a woman who showed me kindness that I had never experienced before. This relationship was different because we prayed together, and she introduced me to her parents, who were pastors. Meeting Mom Alexander in Minersville was life changing. There was no judging, only keeping it real for me. She said, "Daughter, I know you know you will not be able to stay in this lifestyle for much longer. God has a need for you in a much larger scale." I remember saying, "Mom, I know! He keeps waking me up!" Through my years of transition to learning my spiritual self, I completed graduate school, receiving a master's degree in public administration and human services with a concentration in counseling.

Pause break!

When I said God is no respecter of a person, it is so true. Even in my condition, he still used me to minister to others. My family was consistent with weekly attendance at Sunday church services, Bible study, and other church events. My Pastor at the time knew the lifestyle I lived. I never denied it, but I knew God was calling me from it.

"We all sin and fall short of the glory of God!" As you are in transition, remember: if He can use a donkey, He surely can use a sinner like you and I.

♦

I received a call from my pastor requesting a meeting with the elders. Remember, this church house failed to acknowledge their sins, and often looked and commented on the sins of the church family.

He said, "Minister Tammy, we are here to ask you a question?" Being polite and respectful, of course my comment was, "Okay!"

Pastor began the meeting with the inquiry. "Are you currently in a relationship with a woman?" I was in disbelief that he would even put me in front of the elders with this question when he already knew the answer. I knew and everyone else knew of his candor of relationships with the female congregation. It most definitely did not impede upon how God was using him to draw others in.

Nonetheless, my reply was, "Pastor, I have informed you of what God had been doing with my transition because we have been speaking about it." What happened next was so unbelievable. Pastor DJ stated, "I am not aware of such a thing. This is the first I am hearing of this."

I became angry and disgruntled. I held my composure as much as I could. My Spiritual mother was in the room at the time giving me the eye contact of encouragement to hold my head up. I walked out of the room, never to walk through those church doors again.

Sista Girl, *I wish someone would tell the good ole saints at the church house that they are sinning every day but have the nerve to look at someone else's sin as greater than theirs.*

My partner and I prayed. She held me as I cried more. My family rallied around me. I was in such a state of disbelief that continued over several months. What was consistent was hearing God's voice that I was the chosen one to help set the captives free. Needing the continued spiritual guidance and healing, God directed me to attend services led by Mom Alexander. I was under the covenant of love!

Sista Girl... *one thing is for sure and two things for certain, when God has a plan for your life, He will open up doors that no man can shut, even a sinner, as you are.*

With God's continued support to guide me, I was given the assignment to preach. My sermon focused on "Lean Back" into God's unchanging hands. The Church of Broken Pieces of Philadelphia, Pennsylvania welcomed me with open arms, as God used me in a mighty way. Chains were broken, and I was being set free. My path of transformation continues with ministering about healthy lifestyles. It is the mending of my heart as a willing servant to acknowledge the trauma endured by the word of the church as a child.

My personal relationship with God became so much clearer for me. We all have these relationships with others, but the question is, are they season, reason, or lifetime relationships.

My personal/intimate relationship ended with EM, as difficult as it was, and she and I remain friends until this day. When God calls you from the thing, He knows the plans are good.

Sista Girl, *know who you are! Let God change you and not people. He is the greatest transformer. He is the I Am, the creator of the heaven and Earth. What more could he do for such an obedient, devoted child of his?*

Church folks can devastate you, but remember, the One and Only Transformer will put your life back together again. His grace is sufficient!

Now, I am a happily married woman to an amazing husband, and we have several children and a host of grandchildren! Did I mention God fulfilled my dreams after several journeys through life with him, her, and them? I was just a little girl searching for love in all the wrong places. Daddy God restored my faith and my belief that love was possible. He allowed me to see that we are all fallible human beings, but with His grace, we can see clearer. Nobody has the capacity to define you.

Sista Girl…. Did you hear?
He blessed *YOU!*
He blessed *YOU*!
Have you forgotten
your commitment
to Him?
To change,
to grow,
to become
all he needs
YOU to Be
for those
that are coming!
Get in position
through your
commitment!
DO YOU KNOW YOU ARE BLESSED!

By TM(C)12/20/03

Tammy Moody

About Tammy Moody

Minister Tammy Moody gave her life to Christ as a child and renewed her vow to God in 1989 after years of drug and alcohol abuse, broken relationships, and misguided information. Moody is the owner and founder of God Future & Associates, a faith-based company providing counseling and other services to youth and adults. She received her Bachelor of Science in Human Services with a concentration Project Development and her master's degree in Human Services with a concentration in Counseling Drug & Alcohol, Family, and Youth. Mrs. Moody also attended Liberty Theological School. Throughout her career, she helped to reunite over 100 children with their mothers and fathers and has assisted over 150 at-risk youth with getting out of the juvenile system. Mrs. Moody is happily married to her Boaz, Chef David Moody. She has the pleasure of raising their (adopted) son and her granddaughter, which brings them so much joy and happiness. She assisted her husband in opening their catering business called 1st Tri Caterers, where they serve the Tri-State region with Godly love and great food! Mrs. Moody is not foreign to hard work and commitment. She believes it takes God to be right there in the center of all you do for you to achieve your desires.

"I forgive on apologies I will never receive!"

LaTesha M. Sam'i-Melton "The Born Child" ♦ *V1*

FINDING ME

Carla Cain

I have endured,
I have been broken,
I have known hardship,
I have lost myself.

But here I stand,
Still moving forward,
Growing stronger each day.

I will never forget the harsh lessons in my life.
They made me stronger.
(simplereminder.com)

As I stare out my window looking at God's wonderful creation and understand that I am a part of that creation, I'm trying to figure out at 52 years old how and when did I get so lost. When did I become so broken that I didn't know if I could ever be put back together again?

At the age of two, I lost a very important part of myself. I know at that age, people might ask how did you lose a part of yourself? You see, my father was shot and killed by his best friend, who was playing with a gun in the back seat of the car my father was in. So that special first man I should have had in my life was now gone. I never got a chance to know him or feel his love. My mother had a difficult time dealing with my father's death, so one of my father's sisters took me until I was five so my mom could have time to get herself together. My father's family is big and very close, so I had plenty of people in my life to make me feel loved. Once I went back home with my mother, I still spent a lot of time with my father's family, but as I got older, we started growing apart. I was no longer included in all family get-togethers, which left me feeling alone.

Growing up with my mother's family was a little difficult because people thought I thought I was better than them, so they would say mean things to me. To make up for losing my father, his family would give me whatever I wanted, even if I didn't ask for it. So, as I got older, my family called me mean and hurtful names. My mother and grandmother would tell me to stop crying about the things they were saying. During those times, I wished I had my father to tell me everything was going to be alright as he wrapped me in his arms.

My stepfather came into my life around six, and he would give me anything I wanted, but we still weren't close. My mother and stepfather were together for a while, but things started going bad because he was abusive. The abuse affected me emotionally and mentally. I had to learn to hold those emotions in because I had no one to protect me or listen to my feelings. So again, I felt lost and alone, and I could hear the pieces of me falling. That's when I learned to smile and pretend to be happy. If my mom was happy, so was I.

Eventually, my mother left my stepfather, and again it was me and her. But that did not last long because she met a guy that caused my whole life to shatter. At around eight years old, the sexual abuse started and continued until about age 12. The abuse started first by him just watching me as I was showering, then he started touching me. I hated going home, so I would do things in school to get detention. That way, by the time I got home, my mother would be home from work. Since I did not have anyone there to protect me, I turned to food as my comfort and way to cope. When I started gaining weight, I thought by gaining the weight he would stop abusing me. Even though that did not work, food was still my coping mechanism. The weight gain caused people and family to call me fat, but I would just hold in the tears and put on a smile.

My mother was so focused on her relationship that she never noticed my grades dropping and me getting into trouble in school. Then at age 11 my mother got pregnant with my little brother, so any attention I was getting was going to go to him. Again, I felt lost and alone. By 12, I had had enough and told my mother about what was going on. She said we would go to the police the next morning, but to my surprise by the next morning everything had been my fault. Apparently, that evening she had talked to him, and he convinced her it was my fault. That really caused me to be numb to the world. I knew then that I was all alone in it with no kind of protection. My relationship with my mother changed for the worst. If she didn't care about me, why should I care or worry about her?

Life had truly changed for me. I no longer considered myself a child because of the things I had been through. Me and my mother argued a lot and she had me seeing a therapist for my negative behaviors because, as always, it was my fault. It got so bad that one day I came home from school and there was a suitcase packed at the door and my therapist was there to take me to a youth shelter. I was in the shelter for two weeks and then put in a foster home. Again, I felt unwanted and thrown away like trash. I ended up leaving the foster home and going to my grandmother's house when one of the other residents threw scissors at my back. I stayed with my grandmother for a while before I ended up going back home with my mom.

By this time, I was 16 and had gotten pregnant, but my mother made me terminate the pregnancy. It left me even more numb to the world, and I had no one to talk to, so I bottled up my feelings, put a smile on my face and kept moving. It was just another painful experience in my life that left me scarred mentally. Six months later, I got pregnant again and gave birth to my daughter at age 17. The pregnancy caused more weight gain, so the name calling never stopped. My mom and I still had arguments and she would put me out only to have the cops bring me back because she told them I ran away. I shut out the world and felt so invisible, but I had my daughter to love and be loved by.

Even though me and my mom where still having our problems, I still longed for her love.

My mom would have these expectations of who and what I should be and even though I knew they were high expectations, I still tried my best to reach them. Of course, I was never good enough, and she would belittle me every chance she got, which made me feel even worse about myself. The relationship I was in did not help me and my mom's relationship because it was unhealthy, but I thought I was in love. I accepted his cheating and lying, and I still tried to make things work and hold on to him because I wanted and needed to be loved. Some of his behaviors I blamed myself for and tried to figure out ways to fix them. Because I was trying so hard to hold on to this unhealthy relationship, I attempted suicide twice, all because I thought I was in love and couldn't handle the thought of living without him. The one time my mom was there for me, all I can remember was the negative things she had to say. I was so lost and couldn't find myself. I was 20 and had my 2nd child, a son, and had walked away from an unhealthy relationship.

Shortly after the breakup, I ended up in another relationship with an older guy, and I thought this relationship would be different because he was more mature. By our third year, I thought I finally found the love I longed for and was pregnant with my third child–a little girl–which we were so happy about. He started cheating just like the others, so our relationship ended and again I was alone. Three years later, I met a guy through a friend. At first, I was avoiding him, but it seemed like everywhere we went, he was there. Come to find out, my friend was talking with his friend, so that's how he was always where we were. We started talking and three months later decided to be a couple.

Towards the end of our fourth year together, I was pregnant with my 4th child, a little boy. Things started getting rocky between us during my pregnancy after I broke both ankles at eight weeks pregnant. Because I was pregnant, they kept me in my cast longer and when they removed them; I was restricted and couldn't do a lot of things he wanted to do. Plus, I was further along in my pregnancy and just didn't feel like it. One Easter Sunday morning, he came in from work and said he was leaving, so I thought he just didn't want dinner with my family and was going to one of his friends. Then I realized he was packing his stuff. I tried talking to him, but he wouldn't say anything. He finally left, telling me he would come get the rest of his stuff when me and the kids weren't home. I couldn't cry because I just felt numb, so I gathered the children and went to my mother's for dinner, but here I was, 28 years old with four children.

When the numbness wore off, the tears started flowing, and I cried for days until the tears stopped. I thought to myself that if he wanted to stay, he would have, and come to find out he was cheating with someone at my job throughout my pregnancy. That took the wind out of me and once she found out I knew, she would drop notes on my desk, leave notes on my car, and would have her friends say things to me. It got so bad we had to have a meeting with HR in which we both got warnings, even though I did not respond to any of her actions, so I knew it was time to change jobs.

The first year after our breakup, I kept a smile on my face when he would come to visit his son, even though I was crying on the inside. My life turned upside down once again, and I had no one to lean on, not even my mother. During this time, I had to take on a second job just to make ends meet and leave my children home alone with the oldest, who was 14. My mom lived right across the street, but she did not help with anything. She would just call me and tell me everything that was going on at my house. One time she called, and I asked her to go clear all the kids away from my house. She replied, "They're not my kids, I'm not going down there." Well, my daughter ended up pregnant at an early age, and my mother was the one who told me because she had heard it from someone else.

She was like, "You don't even pay attention to your kids to know that your daughter is pregnant. What kind of mother are you?" My life was still spiraling out of control, and I could not manage my finances, which caused me to go crawling back to my mom. She had a lot of stipulations, and that made me and my children to feel we were in lockdown. My mom and I once got into an argument about something the kids did, and it got so heated that she said, "I wish I never had you." That statement cut me to my core, and I knew I couldn't let my children live like this, so I worked and saved up my money to move, but never told her. The day we moved, my mother stood in the middle of the street and called us every name in the book. She started throwing the rest of our stuff out the door, and that day, she ruined her relationship not only with me but her grandchildren. We didn't talk for over a year.

I was now in my early 30s, and my life was still unmanageable; I couldn't keep a relationship, I was working but wasn't bringing in enough money, and still did not know how to manage my finances. I lost another home and had to ask my mom once again for help. This time it was a little easier because she was getting ready to move into an apartment because she decided she did not need to be in that big house by herself. Of course, she charged me rent. One day I came home from work and there was a for sale sign in front of the house. The house sold quickly, and we had 30 days to find a place to live. Luckily, I got the money together and moved out on the 30th day. My mom had no care or concern that we almost ended up homeless.

In my early 40s, I now had a house for several years, a decent job, and had purchased a new car–something I have never done before–and my life began crumbling once again. I lost a great job, my car got repossessed, and bills started piling up. I could not seem to get help anywhere, even from friends and family who I never hesitated to help when they asked, so with the little money I had, I tried to make sure the kids had food. Things started getting turned off and we would stay in the house during the day and go to my daughter's and sleep in her living room at night. It had been a year in a half already and it seemed like I was on a blacklist because I could not find a job at all. Once the water was shut off, the landlord found out and once again we were evicted. Somehow, even without a job, I was able to find another place and moved in two days before I was to be locked out of the other house. The new landlord was nice enough to keep the electric in his name and worked with me on the rent.

My luck was finally turning around. I found a job that I didn't apply for. They came looking for me. I didn't have to interview or anything. They just asked when I could start. I still could not manage my finances though and would "rob Peter to pay Paul" as my grandmother would say. Overall, my landlord was super nice because he always took what I had, and this lasted for several years until he just could not do it anymore and had to take me to court for eviction. What gave me a little comfort was that all my children were grown, and my last child was leaving for college, so the move was less devastating than all the other times.

Working at the job that came looking for me helped start the change in my life. Even though I had to move in with a friend who did not charge me to stay, and all my belongings were in storage, life was going great. I had a job working with women, teaching them how to change their lives for the better. I had to teach a trauma group that I initially did not think I could do because I never dealt with my own trauma. I followed the generational curse of cleaning myself up, sweeping things under the rug, putting a smile on my face, and never talking about it outside the house, so how was I going to teach the women something I could never do? Reluctantly, I started teaching the classes, and we started working on the feelings that the abuse caused us. Even though I was the leader of the group, I did all the assignments and took part in all the activities. By participating in the feeling activity, I learned I felt angry, afraid, detached, embarrassed, frightened, guilty, helpless, hopeless, and my list went on and on. I realized I never dealt with anything because I bottled everything up. When you put names to feelings, it is easier to deal with, so as I was teaching my clients to deal with theirs, I was dealing with my own, and trust me, those classes took a lot out of us, so it was something we could not do every day.

During that time, we worked on forgiveness and that was the hardest thing for me because how could I forgive someone that had taken so much from me and how could I forgive someone who did not protect me when I needed them? The more I thought about forgiveness, the more I understood that forgiveness is not for the other person. It's for you. I taught my clients that forgiveness allows you to let go of the stuff that was holding you back. I spent years holding on to my abuse issues, which caused me to blame others and even myself. Next, I taught them to identify where they fit in their family structure, and for me starting out as the only child, my mother had no one to lean on but me. Then my brother came along, and I still had to be that person to lean on. Next, I taught acceptance, which meant accepting people for who they are and not what we want them to be. That was the eye opener for me–learning that my mom would never be the person I wanted her to be, and it's okay. Don't get me wrong–when we talk about accepting a person for who they are, it means we can't expect them to do something they were never taught to do. Everything I thought my mom should have been doing, she didn't because she was never taught by my grandmother, and my grandmother was never taught by my great-grandmother. That's what we call a generational curse.

Learning to put words to my feelings and learning to accept people for who they are gave me a better outlook on life. It then allowed me to work on my self-esteem, which means I stopped worrying about what people were saying about me. Now, it took a while for me to get there, and sometimes I still think about what people say and how they treat me, but I don't allow it to have control over me. Working with the women on taking back their power allowed me to do the same. I slowly took back my power and refused to allow anyone or anything to hinder that. But during all this time, my life was still chaotic, because even though I had control of my life, I still didn't have control of my finances, and I lost my storage unit with all my family's stuff. I was devastated; all my son's trophies and metals were gone, all my family pictures were gone, little trinkets I collected over the years–everything was gone. I talked about it with my clients so they could see that life happens for everyone, but we must talk about it, deal with the feelings, and move on. I realized everything I lost were material things that could be replaced, and if I was trying to start fresh, then the old things must be left behind.

By this time, my mom was living with my sister. We had an okay relationship, and I was still living with a friend. Since my friend did not charge me rent, I was just spending money with no regards to saving. Eventually, my friend took a job offer and needed to relocate, so again, I was without a place to stay. I knew my sister had an extra room, so I asked if I could stay with them. They discuss it with my mom, and she agreed I could move in. At first it was an okay arrangement, but we were out in an area where you needed transportation, and that was the one thing I didn't have. Since me and my mother worked at the same location, I reluctantly asked her for rides to work.

I felt like I was a boarder confined to my room with my TV and bed. It was hard doing food shopping because I had one shelf in the pantry where I had to store my own pans and dry foods, because I could not use my mother or sister's pots or pans. That left me with no room for anything. I had one little drawer in the bottom of the refrigerator and no spot in the freezer, but I dealt with the situation and was determined to try to get myself out of it. It was hard because they divided everything equally–rent, electric, water–so for one bedroom, I was putting out almost $800 a month. At one point, my youngest had to come home and had to share the room with me, so then they wanted to split the bills to include him. Since he wasn't working, I had to pay it. I did what I needed to do to keep the peace because, as usual, things were getting rocky with my mom, and my sister and her husband decided they were not going to renew their lease. One day, me and my mom had a big blowup regarding riding to work because she waited until 11 at night to tell me she was not going to work, which caused me to have to call out of work due to not having time to find a ride. When I asked her why she waited so long to tell me, she went off and said everything she seemed to be holding in since I moved in and that was the last straw for me. My son had left and was staying with a friend, got himself a job, and we decided to find a place together.

Which leads me to now: I'm in my early 50s and have been roommates with my son and his fiancé for several years. Me and my mother now have a decent relationship because again I've learned that she will never be the mother I need her to be, but I respect her for the woman she is. I no longer try to live up to her expectation of me and learned to make my own. Me and my mother have never discussed the abuse and at this point I think I understand her actions more than she does. She was only doing what she was taught from one generation to the next, but I wanted to break that cycle with my children. I learned I can't control the situation, but I can control how I handle my reaction to the situation.

A couple of years ago, my mother had a stroke and even though we don't have a strong mother-daughter relationship, I was right by her side. I won't say my mom is a bad person–she is just who she is, and I can't, nor do I want to change her. For me, I had to understand that the sexual trauma was not the only trauma I experienced in my life. All those evictions, lost relationships, lost jobs, and other events were traumatic experiences that I never dealt with, and they all just kept me in a crazy cycle in my life. I had to admit that first. First, I had to identify the part that I played in those scenarios and then figure out what I could have done differently. I had to take a moment to look at myself, which is something that is difficult for anyone to do, but when I really sat with me and started understanding me, life changed more.

So here I am, 52 years old, and I can finally say that I've found myself. Really finding me happened not just because of my past or because I took my lessons from each of those situations. Life changed for me on October 2, 2020 when I died. On September 19th I was diagnosed with COVID, which caused me to develop a massive pulmonary embolism. By the time the paramedics got to me, I had no pulse and very low blood pressure. I survived that traumatic experience because of all I learned from the other situations, but one thing that brought me through was my mom telling me she loved me. It took literal death for me to finally hear it, but I'm okay with that. Now, she tells me she loves me on a daily basis, which was really the only thing I wanted from her.

Now, I'm not lost. At the age of 52, I found me.

Through it all, I found me.

I AM ME & I LOVE ME.

Carla Cain

About Carla Cain

Carla was born and raised in Wilmington, Delaware. She is a single mother of four biological children but has about a total of 10 children that consider her a mother figure, and is a proud grandmother of eight. She received my Bachelor of Science in Human Services from Springfield College and continued for her Masters in Human Services with a concentration in Mental Health but was unable to complete due to battling Non-Hodgkin Lymphoma Cancer. Her desire is to go back and finish. Carla has worked 20 years at a woman's correctional institution in a substance abuse program helping women change their lives. She is a helper my nature any and everywhere she goes. Carla is learning to walk in her purpose even if she doesn't always understand it because God does, and that's all that truly matters. Her family is my world, but today, *she loves herself more.*

"There's always a lesson in the still of the morning."

Virginia A. Clark, "A Mother's Worst Nightmare" ♦ *V1*

WHEN GOD REVEALS, WE GOT TO DEAL

Brenda White-Jordan

Has anything ever happened in your life that caused you to pause and think about the true meaning or realization of something that you have known for a while? It's like flipping a switch and the light bulb suddenly comes on! That's essentially what happened to me one Saturday night after an intense argument with my husband.

From as early as I can remember, my mom would call me Mother Teresa because she said I wanted to save the world. She was correct; I was always advocating for someone else, and I felt as though I was carrying the weight of the world on my shoulders. I finally realized that I couldn't save the world, but it took me two divorces and a rocky third marriage to figure that out. When I sat down to write this chapter, I struggled immensely. This was the first time that I actually wrote an account of my life through an introspective view. As I talked to myself about revealing my innermost feelings, I rested on the premise that this simply is not about me, but more about what my life lessons will do to help someone else who may go through the same or similar situations. James 1 talks about the trials that come with being good and how they are like taking cough syrup; it may not taste good but ultimately, it will be good for you.

I heard it stated before that life is like an onion; you have to peel back the layers and some of the layers will make you cry. Early in my life, I thought as most children did. I had the idea of getting married, having children, and living happily ever after. I grew up in a Christian home where we went to church regularly. We were taught to get an education or a trade and work hard so that we could provide for ourselves and our family. My dad's famous saying was, "I don't mind helping you, but you gotta want to help yourself first." I grew up knowing all the right things to do, but it was important to me to find out for myself. I was the child that needed to touch the iron to see if it was hot. Taking someone else's word for it was just not enough. I believe that we all learn in three different ways: through trial and error, through the experiences of others, and what I have learned to be the safest and most effective way, which is through the scriptures.

Lesson 1: I am not the child that didn't have both parents in the home, that wanted for anything, and didn't have a spiritual background. I had what looked like a great start to achieving all my goals. I graduated high school at age 17, having already completed my cosmetology certification and passing my State Board license on the first attempt. I enrolled in junior college, working in a salon and waitressing part-time. Then real life happened. I began to meet new people outside of my family and church family. I was pretty much sheltered from the havoc in the world up to this point and I was clearly ill-prepared to handle the type of people and influences I would later encounter. I learned early on that everyone that is in your boat certainly is not rowing with you. These lessons were hard and difficult for me because I was raised to be honest, truthful, and to treat people the way you want to be treated. I had to learn the hard way that just because you are good to someone doesn't mean they'll be good to you. I found myself on the street, smoking crack cocaine and ultimately ending up in a rehabilitation center by the age of 20.

My parents were very strict and although I had graduated high school and was working two jobs, I had a curfew, and had to be home by 11 p.m. and no later than 11:30 p.m. Unbeknownst to me this structured life would later save my life. I resented my parents for many years because of their strictness. I blamed them for many of my early self-destructive behavior. I rebelled against almost everything they taught me. When my dad told me, "If you can't be home at a decent hour then, don't come home at all," that's exactly what I did. They gave me all the tools I needed to be successful, but I simply didn't apply them to my life.

Lesson 2: After moving from home, I did everything I was big and bad enough to do. I dropped out of junior college, leaving behind a 1.19 GPA. When I returned to school 25 years later and looked at my transcript, I couldn't believe I had an 8 AM class that I completely flunked because I never even remembered having it. My life was spiraling out of control. By this time, I had met my daughter's father, who would later be my first husband, and that was my first introduction to crack cocaine. I was open to trying new things. I smoked marijuana before and drank a little, but it was never a problem. I didn't like snorting cocaine or putting anything in my nose, but I was definitely trying to keep up with the company I surrounded myself with. I was introduced to it through smoking in a joint. I did not know the effect that this drug would have on me. It had just hit the streets and cost about $10 like marijuana, but we didn't realize that it would give you the urge to purchase another and then another until all your money was gone. This wasn't a plan for myself or anyone at the time, I'm sure, but that's why it swiftly ravaged through so many communities. This was in the late 80's and it was new to everyone. Again, my mom tried to warn me about the company that I was keeping, but I insisted on testing the waters. This time went swiftly, but it was a very dangerous time for me. I found myself pregnant, back at home, and noticeably addicted to drugs. My parents were very proactive in attempting an intervention, but again, I had to go through it on my own.

One Friday night, I found myself in a store's storeroom where my daughter's father worked the overnight shift. We would get high in the back of that store when there were no customers present. Shortly after I began smoking, I felt my insides open and blood run down my legs. I was having a miscarriage. The sad part about this memory is that I recall sitting on the stool pushing but still looking for him to bring me more drugs. I only cared about the drug at that moment. I don't remember feeling pain at all, but the urge to smoke was so powerful.

it's an unexplainable experience that I will never forget. I'm not proud of it, but it was that experience that helped me to evolve into the person I am today. I'm thankful that I'm able to reflect upon that time and be fully relatable to anyone else going through the same or similar situations. That and other experiences I went through over the years caused me to go back to school and work with so many charitable organizations. I can relate to people on any platform because of my personal life experiences.

I recall a time, after going to drug rehab and attending church service, repenting and asking for forgiveness. One of our older members said to me after that service, "Don't you ever do that to your parents again." I was devastated but never forgot it. I tell the young people that are trying to get themselves together and going through, just because someone calls you a thing, doesn't mean you have to answer to it! I was coming out of a situation and instead of getting encouragement, I was getting scolded. Again, that experience helped me like many other responses I've gotten through the years on what I shouldn't do.

After this ordeal, I went to my parents and told them I needed help. I looked within myself, and I remembered a Christian girl from the good side of the tracks with the bright future, and I was not her. I learned in rehab that people with addictions will have three different bottoms: jail, institution, or death. Sadly enough, many of my friends chose the latter and are no longer with us. Thank God I survived that very trying time in my life with prayer and a very supportive family. After reconnecting and both me and my daughter's father went to rehab, we eventually got married and had a beautiful daughter, who is now 32 years old. Although crack cocaine was no longer a factor, we were using marijuana and alcohol, and Christ was nowhere in the picture. When things went awry, we had nothing to stand on. In times of turmoil, you can't reach for something that is not already there.

The next few years glided by. I found myself single with a child, simply existing and not really living. I was still smoking marijuana and sometimes drinking, but those were not my drugs of choice, so I didn't feel like it was a problem. When I met husband number two, he appeared to be a decent person. His sister and I were best friends, and our family backgrounds were similar. After dating a short while, he proposed, and we were getting married. I was still trying to do the right thing because of my Christian background. However, I knew he had some issues with drinking because we already had a few spats along the way. I remember calling off the wedding in December and his sister pleading with me that she didn't want anything to happen to her brother, so to please stick with him. There I was, Mother Teresa, feeling like I could save the world, not realizing that you can't save someone that doesn't want to be saved. I needed to be saved myself. That marriage lasted all of six months. Really, it was more like two weeks since we argued profusely on the honeymoon in June and separated three times before Christmas. Here I was again, knowing the right thing to do but doing my own thing instead. What we want is not always what we need and what we need is not always what we want.

Lesson 3: Fast forward to today. My husband, Charles, and I actually met when I was in the seventh grade when he visited my home with my uncle, who was my dad's youngest brother. My dad was the oldest of twelve, so when my mom started having children, my grandmother was also having children at the same time, so we were close in age. Because of our closeness in age, my uncle grew up more like a brother to me than an uncle. Charles and I tried dating on and off in high school and even after high school, but things never worked out in our favor. In high school, because of my parents' strict rules, there was no dating. We tried connecting right after high school, but we both had other things going on. Now, you would think that after all those trials and errors, I would finally get it right. After being separated for a few months, I was headed to Food Lion one Sunday morning to get some drinks to take to our first of the month dinner our church was having to celebrate the birthdays that month, and I bumped into Charles, who worked there. We talked briefly, eventually exchanged numbers, and met up to talk again. By this time, we had both been married, had children, and were both going through a separation and divorce. Over the next seven years, we would move in together with our blended family. He had two beautiful daughters and a handsome son.

Charles and I continued to battle our own demons with addictions and alcohol. We were still casually drinking, until Charles and I had a huge fight one night when he came home intoxicated, and I told him it was going to either be me or the alcohol. Charles stopped drinking but we continued to smoke marijuana casually. We decided to take a job working together to pull things together. That job required us to take random drug tests, so we agreed we would not choose a substance over our lives. We decided that would be it for the smoking and were determined to pull our lives together.

We continued to struggle in our relationship because many of the prior issues were not resolved. We had issues with the children's' mothers, money–you name it, we claimed it. After my daughter graduated from high school, we got married. We were going to church faithfully and Charles got baptized, but we were struggling with living under the same roof. Now that he was baptized into the body, things were different. We felt as though we were both living in sin, so we went to the justice of the peace one Monday night with no prior planning and got married. When I called my parents and told them what we were about to do, they ran down and met us. My dad actually paid the $50 cost of the magistrate to perform the ceremony. Our family insisted on giving us a little reception at my mom and dad's house, but I really wasn't looking for anything because, at that point, I just wanted to do the right thing. I remember my cousin, who had also been married twice already, approaching me on the porch with a question.

He said, "What do you think is going to make this time different?"

My response to him was, "Because we are equally yoked, being of the same faith and belief." That was a great response, but I didn't fully realize the magnitude of that statement. Over our next few years of marriage, we would disagree and even fight over any and everything. Charles still battled drug addiction, and I found myself angry and distant. One Fourth of July, he got into an altercation with my nephew, causing us to have to go to court and me getting a restraining order against my husband. Eventually, we were able to mend our family back together with counseling and much prayer. Over this period, I would do my clients' hair and listen to and help them through many relational issues, from a daughter confiding in me about her mother's boyfriend abusing her to a friend who was planning to separate from her husband of 19 years. I helped everyone else to mend their relationships, but I was silently suffering with mine. I tried everything I thought, even returning to school, acquiring three degrees within five years in the human services counseling field, graduating with honors. With all these dynamic things going on in my life, I was still trying to survive in my own relationship. I returned to school because I had been helping people look beautiful on the outside for decades, but I realized that no matter how good people looked on the outside, what they ultimately needed was to be healed on the inside. Those people that I talked to about were in fact me.

The Epiphany: After years of struggling in my relationships, highlighting scriptures in my Bible and getting my degrees, I finally had an epiphany, and the lightbulb went off. This night, my husband and I were arguing profusely. I don't even remember what the argument was about. To me it didn't matter; the only thing that mattered to me was that I was right, and he was wrong. My mom called me in the midst of that storm and tried talking to me, but I was in a rage, so I continued to argue my point. My sister was visiting that weekend and she took the phone. What she said to me forever changed my life. I was sitting on the bed with my bible open, full of colorful highlights.

She said, "Sis, turn to Proverbs 14:7."

Go from the presence of a foolish man, when thou perceivest not in him the lips of knowledge.

It did not tell me how to fix my husband, it told me how to fix myself and how I responded. I needed to leave it alone; let it go, stop going back and forth. That was the first time that I ever really stopped and applied a scripture directly to a situation I was going through. That scripture did not tell me what to do for him, but for me. Another valuable lesson that I have learned to use in my life: I can't change anyone's behavior, but I can certainly change my response to that behavior. That was a test that I continuously got wrong, so it kept resurfacing in my life. Now that has become my anthem in every relationship and situation. My joy comes from deep within. It is no longer dependent on external circumstances! People don't always act right, and I don't always act right either. However, when you learn how to respond...whew, now that's a game changer! God always gives us the tools that we need. It's up to us to use them. All my reading, studying, and fixing had been for other people. It wasn't until I read the scripture and applied the scripture to my life that I was able to gain peace.

Whenever you are going through a tough time, just remember to run to God and not from God. Sure, you can learn a myriad of lessons through trial and error, but what I have learned is that you don't always make it out to tell your story. Things are certainly far from perfect in my world, but I'm thankful that today I can say that I can grow through what I go through. I have learned some very valuable lessons about carrying burdens that are not mine to carry. Unfortunately, people experience trauma and act out of a place of anger and hurt. It is not my responsibility to accept or fix their behavior. My sole job in this life is learning how to respond to the situation that is presented to me. The only way that I can effectively do that is to apply the tools I have been given.

We can know a thing all day long, but until we apply it to our lives, it can never help you. I've learned that there's always a price to pay in a relationship and they don't last when someone doesn't pay the price. When we learn, it's not a "me against you" but "us against the problem," then we can effectively do what the Word says and that is to effectively relate to each other. Fight for what you want, or what you don't want will take over. If you don't fight for what you want, you are leaving yourself no opportunity to get what you want! You are taking the play out of the game.

Through my early experiences with drugs, failed marriages, and relationship issues, I have learned that people will constantly try to draw from you when they haven't made any deposits. The situation you are going through is only temporary. Life will force you to do something; it is ultimately your choice as to what you do. I have also learned that life is like a boomerang; nothing just goes into the atmosphere and stays there. What you put out will come back. I have learned to look at challenging moments as a comma and not a period. Application is the key to all things. We can have love for someone, but it won't benefit them until we give it. In my challenging moments, I've learned to pour into something or someone else.

Words are powerful and we damage ourselves with negative thinking! God and self-care are my go-to because I can't pour from an empty cup. My health and fitness are a major priority in my life because health is wealth and without it, we can do nothing. Whatever good thing I learn along the way, I do my best to share. God blesses us so that we can be a blessing to others. We are simply His foot soldiers, a vessel. When I purchased my first home, I helped at least five of my friends and family do the same. I've also learned not to feel guilty about taking care of me! My life is about service. I'm eternally grateful that I've been given an opportunity to experience so many challenges and survive them. I refuse to live a life that is not full of gratitude! Because I know God is my source, I constantly look to Him in all aspects of my life. I spend my days caring for my nephew who has a severe seizure disorder. It is only God that could have allowed me to get three degrees in the Human Services field after a 25-year hiatus from school and giving me a job doing what I was essentially already doing. I can now pour out and give back monetarily and of myself through experiences gained through life and a formal education. I listen to many motivational speakers, and I generally start my day with something uplifting. One quote that stands out stated often by Les Brown is, "You must be willing to do the things that others won't do in order to have the things that others won't have." Life can be hard, and you don't get in life what you want, you get in life who you are. Be true to you! I knew who I was, but life will confuse you if you don't stay focused. My favorite scripture is Jeremiah 29:11. God always knew the plans He had for me, and they were always hopeful and with a bright future. Anyone who takes the time to read my story, I pray you understand that, too.

Brenda White-Jordan

About Brenda White-Jordan

Brenda was born and raised in Chesterfield County, Virginia. She's the wife of Charles Jordan Jr. and has been for the last 14 years. Brenda has one daughter and three bonus children. Brenda is a faithful member of the Petersburg Church of Christ (COC) in Petersburg, Virginia. She holds an Associate in Applied Science with a specialization in Social Work, Bachelor of Art in Sociology, and a Masters in Human Services Counseling. Brenda works as a Mental Health Counselor and is a self-employed Cosmetologist whose hair styles and make up have been seen on shows such as the *Rachel Ray Show*, *The Game*, *People Magazine*, and Black Doctors.org. She is an active member of Baby Buns 4Life which educates and supports families with preemie babies and is also a proud member of Continental Societies, Inc. Tri-Cities, Virginia Chapter – a non-profit, tax exempt, public service organization founded as a national organization in 1956. She loves exercising, reading, writing, cooking, and using her creativity to help others, from creating a hairstyle, making door wreaths, or simply saying something to make others smile. Brenda continues to aim towards and produce excellence in all of her ministry opportunities. She has a heart for people and is a committed prayer warrior. One of her life scriptures is Jeremiah 29:11, "I know the plans I have for you, declares the Lord Plans to prosper you and not harm you, plans to give you hope and a future."

"I took a deep dive into understanding myself and my experiences, and I sought God for complete direction for the furtherance of my life"

Tawana M. Peterson, "Committed to Transformation" ♦ *V1*

IFLY

Tawana Peterson

As the man and woman come together in passions of the burning flesh, their emotions collide through moans and groans of their pleasure and time flies. Through all of this, we are given the power to produce and multiply.

What may last for hours, minutes, or a moment often are periods used to fulfill our inner muse, taking for granted the essence of purpose and overlooking the backdrop of the scene. We get caught up in the excitement, not realizing how quickly this phase brings us to the next.

What does one do when positioned to reflect? What takeaways will hold relevant to the heart and mind? Are there regrets, resentment, confusion, or satisfaction that rise up or stand out to transcend the actions of forwardness? Or does the choice to revert and chase the tail keep us from becoming more than we can see? What will we do with what we've produced?

Daily are the steps we take as we rise with breath in our bodies and the activity of our limbs. How often do we rise with the intent to find purpose for the stage? Given the experiences that are encountered throughout life, we are graced with the mental capacity to manipulate to some degree the outcome of our performance. We get to choose our response to intervention. We have the power to change the trajectory of the story when we become mindful of our existence. And even with that ability, having the humility to recognize the source that's greater. Honor the power that brings us to heights unimaginable.

So when we are weak, we are made strong through the connection to the *greater power*. With all our wisdom, we are made wiser through the illumination of that *greater source*. With all the information, technology, resources, and commerce we have to gain; in an instant, it can be lost if we lose connection to the power source. It's easy to assume all rights, but dangerous for the soul.

While it is said that everything happens for a reason, consideration of the flight is always recommended. Mindfulness is a virtue that helps to bring about change. Focusing on awareness and shedding light to shame. So when I connect to my purpose, iFly.

iFly because I've been given the ability to do so.
From the beginning of lustful intents, the results concluded my glide. Dependent on the sheer ability of living, the observance of my experience brings me to a place to know that I can soar. Fearful at first and full of doubt, my stride wasn't realized until I felt the thrust of challenge. That challenge brought on change, change that causes me to use what I had within to take on the tasks presented.

As on wings of an eagle, iFly, no matter the depth or height of the launch.
iFly because I can do all things through the power that lies within.
iFly because greater is HE that is within me than anything in this world.
And while each moment of time lasts for a spell, iFly because I have been charged to do so.
iFly, uFly, we were all created to fly.

Tawana M. Peterson

About Tawana M. Peterson

Tawana M. Peterson, a native of Hartford, CT, was born on November 24, 1975 to the late Richard L. Hill, Jr. and Bertha D. Holloman Hill. As an undergraduate at Johnson & Wales University, she met and shortly after became the wife of Robert L. Peterson and with Robert, is now a proud mother of five amazing children. As a young wife and mother, Tawana pursued life as an entrepreneur to help support their family. In doing so, became the owner of Smarty Pantz Early Education Center. Beginning in January 2020, Smarty Pantz Education and Resources (S.P.E.A.R.) launched it's consulting for aspiring Early Education Providers. In continued pursuit of supporting children and families, Tawana began to advocate for healthy, long-lasting marriages and is now one of the founders of The Marriage Grit, officially established in August 3, 2018. Although the launching of The Marriage Grit took place in recent years, the mission of supporting and mentoring couples had taken place since the conception of her marriage to Robert in August 3, 1996. Entrepreneurship is life for Tawana as is blood through the veins of her body. Her passion to keep these entities alive is a major priority for hers. Tawana has been commissioned to be a light for human services and intends on fulfilling this call through everything that she puts her hands on.

"The healing journey is a never-ending journey, and there's no correct way to go about healing."

Naysia Fils-Aime, "Breaking the Cycle" ♦ *V1*

DEAR QUEEN

LaTesha M. Sam'i Melton

Dear Queen,

Fix your crown! You have endured *enough*. Now is the time to *see* you, *hear* you, and *be* you. That part of your past that held you back before will no longer be a factor in how you move forward. Take this moment right now and just *breathe*! Sometimes we need to hear a kind word or see a friendly face. I hope my kind words to you motivate, inspire, and uplift you.

Just like many women, I too have endured *enough*. In the first volume of *Hold the Line,* I shared parts of my story that took me years to unpack. Prior to getting professional help, I could not understand how the actions of my parents affected me the way they did. I grew up thinking that being silent was helping me. I honestly believed if I didn't think about it or talk about it, it didn't exist. Like many of you, I continued on with being what I thought "strong" was.

What I realized is being "strong" has nothing to do with my

silence. Strong is having my voice heard and being my own advocate. You *can* rise out of anxiety. You *can* rise out of depression. You *can* rise out of the dark days where you may feel like life is suffocating you. You *can* still rise out of generational curses. Did you know you can overcome the obstacles? Did you know you can overcome the fear? You no longer need to hear the voices of self-doubt. The power you thought you lost is still within you. The voice you thought you lost is still within you. The fight you thought was yours in the past was not yours. Your fight is now! Understand that *He* designed your journey for you. You hold the keys to your story and your future. Don't hold on to that dark place of the past. You are here! You are at the light you saw at the end of your tunnel. Now come on and walk through. Walk into your greatness! Be that Queen you always were! You just had a detour getting to your destination and guess what? That's okay. At some point as a woman, you may have felt like or heard someone say what being "strong" should look like. That version of "strong" was for them not you! Being strong is also knowing your boundaries and limits and what you cannot do. We take on so much and never think twice about what we are taking on and how it will affect us.

From one Queen to another: self-care is important to our health. YES! Have your moment of selfishness. Take off all the hats that you hold titles to and just be. Too often we don't do what makes ourself happy because we hold on to the titles of being a good wife, mom, daughter, sister, cousin, best friend, etc. Understand that if you are not doing good and being good to yourself, you cannot be good to or for anyone else. You have to take days off work just for you. Not because the baby has to go to the doctor, or because the baby has a school program; take off because you want a nice quiet day at home while everyone else is at school, daycare, or work. Some of you don't know what self-care looks like. Self-care is not something you have to hurt your brain planning for or something you have to pay a lot of money to do. Here, let me give you a few examples I use for my own self-care and notice how most of them are FREE:

- Buying something for me and me ONLY (NO ONE ELSE CAN USE IT)
- Taking a walk
- Listening to motivational podcasts
- Watching my favorite tv show (by myself)
- Taking a nice bath (while playing soft jazz)
- Journaling (this is a big one)
- Treating myself to a 5-star dinner (normally is a steak dinner being that I don't eat beef often)
- Having my favorite desert
- Zumba (or any type of workout)
- Reading books that will help me personally and business wise

Here are some book resources for you. I have read them all, and they were ***all that!***

- *Black Woman Millionaire* by Dr. Venus Opal Reese
- *Women of The Bible for Women of Color* by Urban Spirit! Publishing and Media Company LLC
- *30 Day Journey to Me (A Self Love Devotional)* by Shawniece Moore
- *The Curves of Life* by Robin Black White
- *The Relaxation & Stress Reduction Workbook* (sixth edition) by Martha Davis, Ph.D, Elizabeth Robbins Eshelman, MSW, Matthew McKay,

Ph.D.

- *Awkward Black Girl* by Issa Rae
- *Badass Black Girl* (it's for teens, but I read it) by M.J. Fievre

Now, you may have to read this next part **twice**. From one Queen to another: Get rid of ***all*** toxic people, places, and things that are in your life. This is so, so, so, important. Speaking from experience, I am here to say it is not easy and it is not something you will do in one day. However, it is necessary. Look, some folks are not meant to be in every season with you. I know, I know. Go ahead and say, "What? You don't even know me like that." You are right, I don't know you "like that". People don't like to read or hear this part. Understand that this is a big part of self-care. For way too long, you have allowed people to use you. Yes. *Use you.* The biggest use people get out of others is time. A more specific example of that is allowing someone to waste your time. Have you ever been in a relationship, and you saw all the "red flags" but you stayed in the relationship because you thought maybe the person would change? Then, when the relationship ended, you realized it could have ended years, months, or days ago? Have you ever had people call on you because they knew you would be the one to do whatever they needed? Have you ever stopped what you were doing just to be front and center for someone else? If you have, *stop! You are important and so is your time!* The thing about this is, you must first identify who is toxic in your life. Toxic people suck life from you, want you to put their needs over your own needs, and don't care that you are on a positive path. These people are *toxic,* and you cannot afford to have them on your journey with you or even in your space. Why? Because it's a vibe!

The hardest people to get rid of will be any toxic parents or siblings. Most of the time we have a sense of loyalty to our parents, right? They're our parents. Both will ruin the relationship with you and then act as if they have or share no blame. Now, cutting them off probably won't work like it would for a friend. Here, distance is key. Establish healthy boundaries with them. This may be painful in the beginning, but once they understand you are finally putting yourself first and that you need this for you, it will get better with time.

You are better now than you have ever been. You are on your own journey to greatness.

This is your winning season, so, Queen, let's win! You have worked hard for this. Allow yourself to be just as happy as the person you have imagined yourself to be. Happiness looks good on you. Own it! Don't allow anyone to speak of you in past tense as the person you "used" to be or the person they want you to stay. People will try to keep you in a space that benefit them only because they want you on their level because it works better for them. I am telling you right now, if you are reading this book, you are no longer that person of your past. Don't allow anyone to pull you into their storm.

From one Queen to another: life will bring you moments of uncertainty and darkness. When this happens, hold on to your faith or whatever keeps your mind, body, and soul at peace. If you take nothing from my chapter, take this: trust yourself because *you are amazing*!

Know you can, so when you do, it's all or nothing.

LaTesha M. Sam'i-Melton

LaTesha M. Sam'i-Melton

About LaTesha M. Sam'i-Melton

From Richmond, Virginia, LaTesha is a wife and mother of four. In 2015, LaTesha Founded 3 Nique Girls, Inc., non-profit organization that focuses on positive interactions between mothers and daughters. LaTesha is a motivational advisor using her platform, LM Speaks, to motivate people through their process of healing.

LaTesha is a Certified Community Health Worker and is an active member of the Virginia Community Health Worker Association and National Association of Community Health Workers. LaTesha also serves on the Henrico/Hanover Reentry committee. In addition, LaTesha serves as Vice Chair at Central Virginia Healthcare Association. When LaTesha is not serving her community, she enjoys spending time with her family, reading, public speaking, and traveling.

PENITENTIARY CONNECTION

We are Holding the Line for the Queens on the inside.

If you know of a Queen behind prison walls who may be blessed by the testimonies told in this book, please send me their name, SBI # and the name of the institution to outoftheashes2015@yahoo.com.

This survival guide will be sent right away.

Made in USA - North Chelmsford, MA
1301158_9780983636427
02.28.2022 1423